THE LAST RIDE

MARK CAHILL

Author of the books:

One Thing You Can't Do In Heaven, One Heartbeat Away,
The Watchmen—and the novels, *Paradise* and *Reunion*—
with over 1.6 million in print around the world.

The Last Ride
A Novel by Mark Cahill

Second Printing, January 2019

ISBN 978-0-9891065-2-8

All Scripture verses cited are from the King James Version.

Editing, Layout, and Cover Design:
    Brenda Nickel

Order additional copies at any bookstore
    or at www.markcahill.org.

Also available in e-book format.

Printed in the United States of America

Presented to:

"Set your affection on
things above, not
on things on
the earth."

Colossians 3:2

"I Could Read This Book Again and Again..."

"Wonderful read!! There can be no doubt that the Lord has given Mark Cahill a tremendous desire for 'all men to be saved, and come unto the knowledge of the truth,' a deep love for the 'pure Word of the Lord,' and great courage to 'earnestly contend for the faith which was once delivered unto the saints.' This book addresses the many false teachings rampant in the world today and their false christs that cannot save. It presents the truth of the God of Abraham, Isaac, and Jacob which can only be found in His Scriptures! Time is short. The King of Kings is coming. Are you ready?" —*Tara Rollins*

"This timely book is a fast overview of the Bible that would take months to learn in Sunday school but is condensed into an accurate picture of what history and the Christian life are about. When coupled with the deterioration and seriousness of our times, it creates the sense of urgency to get our spiritual houses in order and be busy about the things of the Lord. He might be coming sooner than any of us think." —*Don Hess*

"An interesting point of observation down through time. Bringing to the attention of the reader how things that were predicted in the Bible actually came to pass, thus showing the reliability of God's Holy Word. Each chapter creates a hunger for the next, concluding in the wrapping-up scenes of this world. Have a nice ride!" —*Dennis Higley*

"This book completely fascinated me and was hard to put down. It is a real eye-opener about the truth of the Bible. The deep love of God for both the lost and the saved jumps off of every page. It shows how God has provided the remedy for our sins, wants our repentance and faith for salvation, asks us to live for Him, and shows us how to recognize the signs of the times. I could read this book again and again and still learn new things, and I plan to do just that." —*Simone Monteith*

"God's tender heart toward His creation and the refusal of mankind to heed His warnings are abundantly clear in each chapter of this book. Mark Cahill presents the simplicity of truth in his fast-paced staccato style, which builds anticipation toward a crescendo that includes several surprises at the end. By contrasting the heavenly and earthly perspectives of history and what awaits the world at the end of time, you will be impacted with the importance of the choices you make in your life today. This book left me in tears looking at people not with earthly eyes, but with the heart of the Lord!" —*Sally Wilkinson*

Chapter 1
The Last Moment

"**It's time. We're about to** be called. You ready?" Crimson said as they began to prepare.

"Not sure," Ivory answered. "Amazing that it has come to this. I never would have anticipated this outcome. How about the rest of you?" he asked as he looked at the others.

"We're all seeing it the same way," Onyx agreed. "But there is no other choice, really. Right is right, and wrong is wrong. Truth is truth, and lies, well, you know where they lead."

"That's all too clear now," Elap replied as it turned quiet. It had been a long time coming.

As they made their final preparations before heading out, Ivory broke the silence, "Remember back at the beginning how fascinating it all was? How much wonder we had? Watching it all unfold right before our eyes? We were completely speechless and enthralled by the magnitude of what was taking place. Remember the awe we had as we tried to wrap our minds around what was happening?"

"Definitely unlike anything we had seen before," Onyx agreed. "We had nothing to compare it to. No way to describe it. It was all completely different, yet so perfectly designed. One marvel appearing as another was exploding on the scene. Miracle after miracle. A sight to behold and never to be forgotten."

"We knew something incredibly special was taking place," Crimson recalled. "But now, we have been summoned. Duty is calling. Our mission is on the horizon, but it should never have been necessary in the first place. Yes, we have an assignment; and we will most certainly complete it."

Silence fell over them again. It was time to go. They paused as if to hold back the inevitable. They knew this would be the point of no return, but the journey ahead must be made. It must be completed. It must be.

Their hesitation allowed them to get lost in the past once more before leaving. Taking a last look around, they recalled the weighty events that had led up to the task at hand. Onyx remembered back to the beginning and how it all began . . .

"Quick! Ivory, Crimson, and Elap. Hurry! The heavenlies are gathering to watch, and you guys don't want to miss this! The anticipation is everywhere around us because nothing the Eternal One does is anything short of miraculous!" Onyx said to his friends.

"Until now it's been the light of eternity, but darkness has appeared. And it looks like things are about to change. Something is about to happen. The suspense is overwhelming! Look! The Spirit of God is moving across the waters. What is He about to do? Oh wow! He is creating!! Oh my! He is making the earth and Heaven. He is having so much fun as He does this. Something very, very special must be going on here because He's creating on a grand scale! And He's speaking light into it!

"Look again! He just separated the darkness from the light and has called them day and night. He must be doing that for a reason. God is light, and in Him is no darkness at all. If this is the beginning of creating the heavens and the earth, I wonder what it will be like in the end.

"Why is He taking so long to make whatever He is making? Why is He pacing Himself as He does His work of creating? My guess is that time will be different down there. It sure doesn't work that way up here. There are so many new and different things coming from God that it will be neat to see how this all unfolds."

"Thanks for your play-by-play, Onyx, but let me step in," Ivory interjected. "Do you see how He is separating the waters by creating an expanse between them? Why, oh why, is He doing that? Looks like Day Two is now finished.

"Under this expanse, the waters are being gathered; and land masses are emerging with seas all around them. I am not sure I understand any of this. Even though it catches me off guard and is hard to comprehend, I know the Eternal God must have a reason for making such an enormous creation.

"Look, fellas! Across the land masses, we see green herbs, grasses, fruit trees, and all kinds of vegetation appearing. Why is He creating all of those things? What purpose could He have in mind for them? To watch how all of this progresses will be incredible to see.

"Now we are at Day Four, and I'm puzzled about why He doesn't just create everything all at once. Since He is God, He is all-powerful and can bring all of this into existence in the blink of an eye. I keep wondering why He is taking so long."

"If we have learned anything by now, Ivory, it is He has a reason for everything He does—and I do mean everything! We will find out in due time. Remember, part of the adventure is the joy of discovering these things. We know the destination will be great, as it always is with the Lord, but let's wait and see how this journey plays itself out!" Onyx suggested to them all.

"Are you seeing what He is doing now? He is hanging things all over the heavens! Lights are illuminating the skies! There is a great light that gives off bright light during the day, which a lesser light then reflects when it is night. The night skies are now twinkling with tiny lights in the far distance. This is completely amazing and so beautiful, all at the same time.

"Look at those bodies of water! It is Day Five, and the Almighty is filling them with whales, sharks, starfish, jellyfish, squid, crabs, lobsters, seahorses, snails, octopus, dolphins, clams, turtles, crocodiles, manatees, alligators, eels, and frogs. Can you see how much fun He is having as He designs all of these animals? Astounding creativity! Incredible design! Their movements are fluid and precise. How unique and different they are from one another! What pleasures to the eyes to see, once again, what He is able to make.

"Now He is making finches, gulls, thrushes, bats, eagles, cardinals, parrots, flies, beetles, insects, dragonflies, and so many more creatures to populate the skies! This is amazing. The beauty is stunning. What color! What agility! What distinctive sounds they make! I know all of those creatures are enjoying themselves; but trust me, the view from up here is much, much better than even a bird's-eye view! Is there more that He will create, or will this be it?

"Well, just as I expected: He isn't done! Do you see all of those animals running around? Lions, tigers, bears—oh my— giraffes, cows, pigs, badgers, mice, chipmunks, dogs, and cats! Animals are scurrying around everywhere! Can anything ever be created that is better than any of these?

"How long will it be before He is finished with this splendid creation of His? And what could He possibly create that would be different from what our eyes see now? But wait! Did you hear that, fellas? What did He just say? *'Let us make man in our image.'* What does that mean? What is man? Keep your eyes wide open because this sounds pretty special!

"And it is! Look at that being He just formed from the dust of the earth! He is amazing! He is eternal! He has a soul. He will live forever. And He is made in the image of His Master. No other thing that God has created is anywhere close to being in this same category. There is nothing He has ever made that is like them. He has made them male and female. He wants them to be fruitful and multiply. My, oh my. What a loving Creator. What a gracious God to make mankind in His own image. I hope they realize how special they are to Him! But now, I think I understand something. It looks like everything He has created was made just for them! They are His special creation!

"God is looking at everything He has made and says it is very good! I know He did all of this in six days, but I am just as curious as you guys are about why it has taken Him so long to bring all of this into being. Why didn't He just speak everything into existence all at once? Why did He create for six days and then rest on the seventh? We know we are going to find out eventually; and boy, will that be something when it is finally revealed!"

"The view from up here is amazing! I wish those two humans could see the panorama we can see from our vantage point," Ivory said, surveying the newness of everything before them.

"It looks like they are the last of His creation, but this will not be the last of His love for His creation," Onyx declared.

"What a glorious week that was!" Ivory exclaimed as they remembered back. "We were so astounded by the power coming from the hands of God. Everything was so intricately and precisely fit together. His goodness and love were on full display. Utterly amazing."

"I often think about that week in the beginning, but especially now that we're on our way," Onyx reflected.

"I'm sure you guys remember what happened to God's perfect creation afterward, right? Can that ever be forgotten? What was supposed to be a heavenly paradise on earth didn't last long before it was spoiled," Ivory regretted.

Chapter 2
Good While It Lasted

"**Hey, guys, do you see** those gardens down there? God sure has thought of everything for His creation. The vegetation is lush and teeming with plants of various kinds. Such vibrant shades of green. What a gorgeous place for mankind to live! They have it so good," Crimson said admiringly.

"God has provided them with all of those trees in the Garden to eat from, but He has just given Adam a warning. I wonder why He did that. Adam wouldn't disobey Him, would he? That would be a foolish move. God said he can eat of every tree in the Garden except from the tree of the knowledge of good and evil. Well, that is pretty simple. There are tons of trees down there. Adam can eat from any of those. No need to eat from the one tree God has instructed him not to eat from. Seems pretty simple to me. Adam wouldn't go against His word, so I am not even sure why God warned him that if he does eat from that tree, he will die? What does *die* mean? We have so much to learn from all of this!

"The generosity of God just continues to astound me. It shouldn't, though. I have seen it time and time again. There is man, and now God has created a woman to be a help meet for him. They are going to be a team! Those two will now become one flesh. Do they even realize how much He cares about them? From our viewpoint, God seems to be crazy about them. I bet they understand that, considering all He has done for them up to this point. Yes, I am sure they will never forget His love for them.

"Look who just showed up, fellas! The evil one himself. The most subtle deceiver of all time has now entered the scene. What is he doing there? What does he want? I guess we can figure this one out. He wants to mess up what God has created somehow. It is all he has wanted to do since he rebelled against God, but what is he scheming to do in the Garden? I wonder who he sees as his prey on this hunt."

"That serpent has the woman in his sights! I literally cannot believe he is talking to her," Elap worried. "Why is she listening? No one should listen to him! He speaks with forked tongue! He just said what? *'Yea, hath God said, Ye shall not eat of every tree of the garden?'* That isn't what God said! He is twisting the words of God. She must know better than to listen to him. God's command to Adam was clear. She and Adam know what God said. They won't fall for the serpent's dastardly plan.

"Now she is conversing with him! Why doesn't she run? Why doesn't she get away? Why won't Adam step up to the plate and do something? This is not the time for a wimpy follower of God. We know the evil one plays for keeps. This is not a game to him. She needs to run and run now, before it is too late.

"Did you guys hear that? The serpent just said, *'Ye shall not surely die.'* That is a bald-faced lie. The father of lies is lying again. It is what he does best. It is frightening to think about what might happen here. She knows what God said, and she knows that what Satan just said completely contradicts God's command. He is enticing her to go against God! What will her choice be? She most definitely has a choice to make, and it is an easy one.

"Obviously, Lucifer isn't finished. He is adding even more to God's words as he says, *'For God doth know that in the day ye eat thereof, then your eyes shall be opened, and ye shall be as gods, knowing good and evil.'*

"The woman knows she must obey God. Doesn't she remember the consequence for sin? It has to be in the forefront of her mind, even though the serpent is giving her reasons to disobey God. She won't—she can't—fall for this deception. Certainly, Lucifer will lose this battle for her heart and mind. We can see it all taking shape from up here, and it's starting to look like bad news. She just needs to trust and follow God here.

"No way! I can't believe she is looking at the fruit! She shouldn't be doing that! It is capturing her eyes. It is easy to tell that her flesh wants that fruit. I sure hope her pride doesn't win so that she wants to be like God. Just obey! Please, just obey!

"Well, that didn't take long. Not only did she just eat of the fruit, but she gave some to her husband! Adam was standing right there with her the whole time. Lucifer saw him, and we saw him. Why did he not protect his lady? Why did he not love her or God enough to step in and end that discussion? Doesn't he care for her? We know he does, but Adam has just made a horrible decision. He was so cowardly, and we know there will be consequences for their disobedient actions. God gave them one simple command. Do not eat from *ONE* tree in the Garden. They have messed up royally. This is not going to end well. Now they will surely die. Not sure what that means, but it looks like we are about to find out. God always keeps His words. He is unchanging. If He makes a promise, He will keep it. And if He promises a consequence, He will follow through. They can bank on that."

Crimson piped in and said, "Isn't it interesting how God first asked Adam if he had eaten of the tree? Since God is all-knowing, He knew the whole time that the woman had eaten of the tree first, so there must be a reason why He asked Adam that question before asking her. I think God did that because He gave the command to Adam and knows that Adam should have protected his wife, and he did not. He failed in one of his main duties as a husband.

"The good news is that the woman answered God honestly, too. That will bode well for her. Always be honest with God. Never hide things. He already knows. Now the woman is going to have a lot of labor when she has kids. Adam will have to work much harder than he ever anticipated. Those consequences are less severe than they could have been. God could have wiped them out, but He didn't. If there is one thing we know, it is the kindness, the mercy, and the compassion of the Most High God. That will never, ever change. That is who He is. It is His being.

"God just told them that they will return to the dust of the earth. That is what dying must be, but they are still made in His image. I am having a hard time figuring out how they are eternal, yet will die. I am sure it will become clear with time.

"Adam just gave his wife the name Eve, and she will be the mother of all the living. They have also been kicked out of the Garden of Eden. They cannot be anywhere near the Tree of Life now that they have fallen into sin. It will be so, so interesting to see how all of this plays out. I'm kind of glad we are seeing it from up here instead of from down there after what just happened.

"We sure hope this will be the last time they disobey the Master; but since He has given them the ability to choose, I guess we will have to wait and see."

After remembering back to the days of the Garden, Elap said, "To watch God's beautiful creation fall into wickedness was just devastating. Everything was perfect at first, and then disobedience corrupted it. Disobedience has always done that."

"And didn't we know that once the devil slithered in the door, he would force it open to every evil under the sun. He thought sin would bring the last of God's goodness to mankind, but God had a door of mercy opened wide to them, until the deluge came and the way of escape was closed," Crimson said.

Chapter 3
Last Chances

"*It sure turned wicked down* there in a hurry, Elap, and we can tell God is going to do something about it. Looks like this experiment is going to be over sometime soon," Onyx surmised.

"Nothing is ever an experiment to God. He doesn't experiment on anything."

"Good point, Elap. The wickedness down there is so great. Even we can see that people's thoughts and imaginations are very wicked just by looking at their actions.

"The Lord is grieved that He has created this magnificent world, and now it is filled with evil. What a dichotomy. It's so clear that He loves all of His creation and adores those who are made in His image; but yet, they have astonishingly decided to walk away from Him. They have chosen to let flesh be their guide instead of their Heavenly Father. What a horrendous choice they have made.

"Oh my, did you hear what God just said? He is going to destroy all that He has created! The earth has become corrupt, and there is so much violence everywhere. We can tell He doesn't want it this way. He has such love for all that He has made."

"Hey, fellas, looks like God isn't done with mankind yet!" Elap informed the others. "There is a man named Noah, and God has found him righteous! Noah is a just man. He is God's kind of guy! God is going to offer him grace and preserve his family. Not only that, but Noah will warn people to repent of their wickedness and turn to God. That is just like God's character, isn't it? He is providing them a way of escape! He so wants to shower more and more of His love on those people down there. I sure wish they could see it from our angle. Now there is hope, and it will be exciting to see where it all goes from here.

"God is having Noah build an ark, but I'm wondering why He is doing that.

"Noah and the gang are doing an amazing job. Look how big that ark is! It appears to be right about 450 feet long, 75 feet wide, and 45 feet high. It is huge! There are three decks in that thing. I guess there is a reason why God is having Noah make it so big. There is so much open space in that ark.

"God is always thinking ahead. I guess that is what being all-knowing can do for you! He wants them to make the ark out of gopher wood, which is highly resilient to rotting. There must be a reason why He has decided they should use that. The pitch they are using will prevent decay and make the ark totally waterproof. It is no surprise to us that God thinks of everything!

"That boat literally cannot capsize, no matter how rough the seas get. There is enough room in there to fit almost 570 standard railroad boxcars, and it can fit around 125,000 sheep! When I am talking huge, I literally mean *huge*!

"Looking over all the earth, there are about 36,000 species of animals down there. God appears to be bringing them two by two to the ark, so He must intend to keep those species flourishing. There are even more of the clean animals coming so that now, there are about 75,000 animals total. A lot of those critters aren't the biggest things I have ever seen! Even the young dinosaurs have plenty of room to move around. There is so much room on that ark for the animals and their food that I don't know what Noah is going to do with all the extra space. You would think God is sending them on a cruise around the world! It's like the ark has its own wildlife park and aviary, complete with dining rooms and exhibit halls! There are so many nooks and crannies to explore on that ship that Noah and his family will be busy from morning to night! Whatever the journey is that they are about to take, they will have plenty of room on board to stretch out!"

"God just told Noah, his family, and all of the animals to enter the ark. Something big is about to happen," Onyx asserted.

"Are you guys seeing what is happening down there? It has begun to rain mightily on the earth. The canopy of water vapor surrounding the earth is collapsing, and the fountains of the great deep are breaking up. Water is coming from everywhere, and it won't be long before the waters begin to rise. Did you also notice what God just did? He shut Noah and his family up in the ark. They and all the animals are now protected from the torrents of water. Why didn't those people who are left behind believe Noah's preaching? Why didn't they understand how kind God is? Why didn't they repent of their wickedness and come running to Him? Now there is water everywhere, and it is way too late for them to be safe within the ark.

"What a flood! The floodwaters just keep rising and rising. The highest mountain tops and peaks are now covered; and as far as the eye can see, it is only water and sky. What is going on? God sure means business when He warns. When He says He hates wickedness, He means He hates wickedness. He despises it. It is anathema to Him. Why didn't they get it?

"All of those people who were not in the ark have now died. No more chances for them to get right with God. All of the animals that were not in the ark have also died. It was literally a worldwide flood. All of them are dead. Those folks are sure not mocking God anymore. They had the chance to trust Him. He graciously gave them time to repent and believe while the ark was being built. His mercies and compassion fail not. When the flood hit, there was no turning back. God's decision had been made; and without fully realizing it, their decision had been made, too. Now they will live out the consequences for their sins and their rejection of God forever.

"Noah and his family are safe, and all of the animals have disembarked from the ark. Now they can be fruitful and multiply.

"Do you see what Noah is doing? He is sacrificing some of the clean animals to the Lord. We can see it is a sweet savor to Him. Noah truly, truly loves the Lord. What a special relationship they have! Finally, the people of earth are back on track with God. It should be smooth sailing from here on out!"

"God just promised this will be the last worldwide flood; and hopefully, it is the last time He will need to get their attention, too," Elap remarked.

Still standing together, Onyx spoke up, "Weren't we thrilled to see God preserve mankind through Noah and his family?! Evil had to be destroyed, but God has always wanted to save. He has always offered terms of peace before judgment. Just His character. But men were so stubborn."

"Yes, and as time moved onward from then, it was amazing to see how rebellious mankind continued to be," Elap exclaimed.

"I agree! Remember centuries after the Flood when we saw the poster child of rebellion? What a battle that was between the forces of evil and the God of light and truth!"

Chapter 4
A Lasting Memorial

"*The goodness of God is* something that *we* already know. What a God!! But since the Jewish people are in Egypt and not their homeland, it is probably time for them to be going back. I hope Pharaoh gets the message; because if he doesn't, things will not go well for him," Crimson declared.

"It is time for an *exodus,* or a departure, to the Promised Land. God made a covenant with Abraham, and He will fulfill it. He always does," Ivory added.

"Are you seeing what I'm seeing? God is appearing to Moses in the burning bush! What a sight! The bush isn't even burning up! God has a love for Moses that is off the charts. I really get the feeling He wants to mold Moses into one of His mighty followers—a mighty warrior for God!

"God just loves men of God who will make a bold stand for Him. He uses them all the time. It's never easy being one of these men. There are always temptations and critiques seemingly at every turn, but we can look down and see that Moses has those humble qualities God wants to use.

"Looks like it is time for the Israelites to leave the bondage of the Egyptians," Crimson remarked. "It also looks like Pharaoh has no desire to let them go. I guess this should come as no surprise. Sinners love to be in power. So it looks like God is going to show out again! I don't know why folks down there just won't trust and believe in Him. Sure seems like it would be an easier way to meander through life. But I guess stubbornness must be one of the bad qualities they inherited from the fall.

"No! He didn't. Please, someone tell me that Pharaoh did not just say that. God sends Moses and Aaron to tell him, *'Thus saith the* LORD *God of Israel, Let my people go, that they may hold a feast unto me in the wilderness.'* And Pharaoh's response is, *'Who is the* LORD, *that I should obey his voice to let Israel go? I know not the* LORD, *neither will I let Israel go.'*

"Doesn't Pharaoh realize this is a game he cannot win? There is like a zero percent chance he can outmaneuver the Lord God of Israel, but he still wants to try anyway? Is he clueless? Is he not thinking straight? If he could see things from our vantage point, he would not make such a foolish statement. Well, if he wants to play chess with the Grand Master that is his choice. This will probably not end well for him. This will be a major defeat. This will be checkmate without even losing a pawn! Let's see how this plays out.

"Uh-oh. The Nile just turned to blood. God is serious. Will Pharaoh take Him seriously? The Nile is Egypt's lifeblood. Everything seems to revolve around that river. The water is now unusable, and there are dead fish everywhere. When the Nile overflows its banks, it provides the most fertile of farmlands. The Egyptians can grow almost anything and everything on those plains. It floods and fertilizes nearly eight miles of land on either side of its banks! No more. The river is blood. The life-giving power of the Nile has now turned to death. Oh my. The hand of God is truly powerful and amazing. One of the gods that Egypt worships is Osiris, the god of the underworld. Amazingly, the Egyptians believe the Nile is his bloodstream. Well, they have all the blood they want now. This god has literally bled to death.

"The Egyptians love their frogs. To them, they are a reminder of the fruitfulness that is coming. There will be a good harvest this year. That is why we see frogs depicted in many of their paintings and amulets. Frogs are, pretty much, sacred to the Egyptians. They are not supposed to kill them. Sadly, they worship the goddess

Heqet, who is depicted as a frog. She assists with childbirth, so they think; and, of course, they have thought wrong.

"So what does God do? Literally, frogs everywhere for everyone! Frogs, frogs, frogs! Here a frog, there a frog, everywhere a frog, frog. People are stepping on them. People are slipping and falling on that slimy mess. They are killing their own goddess. Pharaoh even has frogs in his house! Now the people want them gone. They want one of their deities to disappear! This is fascinating.

"Look! The Lord is causing the frogs to die. The Egyptians are piling them in heaps. The land down there must really stink. It must be very, very humbling to realize that your god really isn't a god; and at the end of the day, he really stinks.

"Now if frogs aren't enough, here come the gnats! Our kind has never liked gnats, so we know humans won't like them either! Those gnats can sting, get into your eyes and nose, and literally be one big irritant! The Egyptians should not have believed in Set, the god of the desert. These gnats seem to number as many as the sands of Egypt. Those folks have to know this is the finger of God working against them, but Pharaoh is one prideful man. It seems like pride is the downfall of most men down there.

"I am not sure why they don't listen, but here come swarms and swarms of flies. They are the blood-sucking kind. This is not going to go well for the Egyptians. Sadly, they worship flies because they represent their god Uatchit. They even make amulets in the shape of flies. Interestingly, none of those flies are messing with the Jewish people or their land. This plague is only for the Egyptians; and it should, one more time, prove to them who the real God is. Will they listen? I am not getting good vibes here because they are not paying proper attention to the God of the universe.

"As we might have guessed, Pharaoh has his own agenda. He is trying to show he is in control. He doesn't want to look bad in front of his people. The problem is that his people want all of these plagues over with! Pride is an amazing thing for those humans. Since he won't let God's people go, here comes a fifth plague. The cattle are now dying. God is showing His power over creation again. But the cattle of the Hebrews are just fine! The hand of God has not touched them. Pharaoh has even sent someone to check out that report. He knows deep down that he is out of his league. He knows he is fighting against the God of the entire universe. Why won't he repent and believe?

"The bull and cow represent their god Ptah and their goddess Hathor. These animals are basically considered sacred. Now what? They have been destroyed. Their god did not show up and defend them. We know their gods don't exist. God is showing them that He is the one and only God of the galaxies. No one else. What more does He have to do to prove it to them?

"Reaping what you sow is an amazing concept. The Egyptians forced the Jews to make bricks for them. Many, many hours dealing with those burning, hot furnaces were not good days for them. Now Moses sprinkles those ashes in the air, and boils have sprung up on the Egyptian people. Those boils do look painful. Even the magicians of Pharaoh cannot stand before Moses because of the excruciating pain those boils have caused. Serapis, the Egyptian god of healing, must have called in sick today because his people are not doing so well! Maybe he can write them a doctor's note or something, but he has failed miserably at protecting his people.

"God is going to get Pharaoh's attention, and He is going to glorify His Name! He deserves the honor and glory that are only reserved for Him. I don't know how much longer these plagues will go on or how bad they will get, but we know what the end result will be: God will be glorified!

"God just let Pharaoh know that if he doesn't obey Him, then much more trouble is coming. He is such a benevolent God. His compassion knows no bounds. All He wants is for Pharaoh to repent and believe. Yet, Pharaoh hasn't to this point. I have a bad feeling here. I think he is going to test the Lord some more. That never works in the long run. It seems, from this bird's-eye view, that people down there don't often think long-term. Always caught up with the here and now. What will satisfy me and my ego today? I sure wish they would live their lives with an eternal perspective in mind.

"The Egyptians have made the mistake of believing in Nut, the sky goddess. Not sure why they believe in her since, many times, the southern part of Egypt has no rain for an entire year! I would think it is time for a new goddess! She is considered the mother of many other gods. Well, I guess it is good to be nice to mom, but this *mom* sure isn't doing much for them!

"A grievous hail is now descending from the skies. This is truly the hand of God. We have never seen anything like this before; and hopefully, we never will again. The hail is destroying the flax and barley of the Egyptians. But that is not all. It is hitting their houses. It is hitting the statues and monuments of their gods that cannot protect them. God is sending them a huge message. His power is on display in a mighty way. Will they listen, or will they continue to tune Him out?

"God is obviously upping the ante because here come the locusts! Not just a few of them, but this is a swarm times a swarm. Look at all of them! They are covering the face of the earth. I am not big on counting, but it sure seems like there are hundreds of thousands of locusts per square mile. Those insects can jump two feet at a time, and they look hungry. This will devastate the wheat and rye crops that survived the hail. We know what this means: there will be no crops for the Egyptians. They will all be gone.

"Their gods Nepri, Ermutet, Thermuthis, and Seth are the gods of their crops. Well, either the locusts ate the crops before they could get there, or they are just having a bad day. We know they don't exist, but I sure hope Pharaoh realizes that at some point very soon.

"The land has become dark. There are so many locusts that they are blocking the rays of the sun! The power of God is showing that He is the One and Only God. Why won't they listen?

"The good news is that Pharaoh has just admitted to Moses and Aaron that he has *'sinned against the LORD your God.'* I wonder if he means it or if he just wants the locusts to disappear. We can't see inside his heart, but I am beginning to wonder. He has been a schemer in the past, so I am not sure I am trusting him here. His past record doesn't bode well for him at the moment.

"People are going to come to the conclusion, one way or another, that God is God. It will either happen while they are on earth, or it will most definitely happen the moment of their last breath when they cross to the other side. Then it will be too late for them to repent and believe. We can tell that is one of the reasons why the Almighty is trying to get their attention. He wants it now, before it is too late.

"Uh-oh. A deep darkness has now come upon the land, and there is no comparing it to the darkness caused by the swarms of locusts. Amon-Ra, or Ra, is the chief deity of the Egyptians. The piercing rays of the sun bring the heat and light they need to grow crops. No sun; no crops. So when Ra rises in the morning and brings his light, people know he is there and he will take care of them.

"Big problem, though. This darkness has now lasted three days! Three very long days. It looks like a thick kind of darkness, almost like you can feel it. What's interesting is there is light in the Jewish region of Egypt! They have light! They can see! Yahweh always is, has been, and will be taking care of His people; and that is no surprise to us!

"Interestingly, we don't know what that darkness feels like. It has been light, light, light for us! Entirely light and nothing but light, so help me God! Light just emanates out of God. It radiates everywhere. We can feel it: the warmth. The elimination of anything contrary to Him, which I am guessing is what darkness represents. I am so glad that we do not have to experience what they are going through down there.

"This is also a judgment against Pharaoh. We can tell it is one reason why he is very bent out of shape. He is the divine representation of Ra on planet Earth. Pharaoh is his man, and he is failing miserably in every single encounter he is having with Jehovah. He is like *zero for nine* right now! He really needs to throw in the towel, repent, and come to the real King.

"Ironically, many of the Egyptians are realizing this, too. They realize this is a losing battle. Their puny, non-existent gods do not, will not, and cannot stand a chance against the Most High. Ra and Pharaoh cannot cut it. The Egyptians were sold a bill of goods. I am wondering how many of them will turn to the true Light Source of the universe?

"What is coming next looks to be the final act of this very serious showdown. The firstborn male is going to die. This will be devastating. This will hit these families very hard. This will paralyze them emotionally. The Lord has said this will be the final plague. There won't need to be any more. This scene will have a lasting effect for generations to come. Their oldest male child, in whom they have invested so much time and energy, is about to move on over to the other side. This is going to be very difficult for both the father and the mother. They are about to realize that their gods Isis, Selket, Min, and Renenutet, the cobra-goddess who supposedly protects Pharaoh, are no match for El Shaddai. Pharaoh is also considered to be an immortal god, as is his firstborn son, but that belief is about to come to a screeching halt. The Almighty God will, one last time, show all of these people who has the power and who does not. This is going to be overwhelming. Literally disastrous. But one thing for sure is that no one—and I do mean no one—will ever forget who is in charge. There is One God. He is the Creator of all. There is none like Him, nor will there ever be. Will these people come running to Him or continue to run away? Two choices: For God or against God. Pretty simple. What will their decision be?

"This plague is very different in a distinctive way, though. The Jews were protected from the other plagues just because of their heritage. This one is different. God will be asking them to do something. They will have to take a step of faith. They don't have to do it. They can assume that God will protect them anyway, but that will prove to be a costly decision. When God says to do something, He means it. No playing around with Him. You may not understand why at that moment—and you may not even want to do it—but if He says it, it is time to obey. Obeying God because of your love for Him will always be the best option to choose. But choose, you must!

"The Jews will need to take an unblemished male lamb and sacrifice it. Interestingly, they must keep the lamb for fourteen days. Why does God want them to do that? They will become attached to it. The kids will love the lamb like a pet. They will grow very close to it, and then it will be sacrificed. This is going to be emotional. This shedding of blood is going to cost them something. They will now have so much more invested in this act of faith in trusting the Lord.

"After the lamb is sacrificed, God has instructed them to put the blood on the sides and tops of their doorposts. Reminds me a bit of the times when there was the shedding of blood in the Garden and also when sacrifices were made after the Ark came to rest.

"It is time. The Lord has gone out. It is time for this plague to commence. As you guys can see, He is passing over the houses with the blood on the doorposts! Those firstborn sons will not die. They will survive. They obeyed the Lord. The sacrificial blood was enough for God to pass over their abode. Wow! Those people need to realize that He also wants to *Passover* their sins, as well.

"The cry is great in Egypt. Every household has been affected. This is too much. This is the end. Pharaoh will finally let the Jews go, and it is about time.

"I guess we should have figured out that Pharaoh wouldn't let loose of that great workforce so easily! Now he is following after them. Not a good move on his part. I think he is about to cross over to the other side.

"Moses is telling the Hebrews, *'Fear ye not, stand still, and see the salvation of the LORD, which he will shew to you to day: for the Egyptians whom ye have seen to day, ye shall see them again no more for ever. The LORD shall fight for you, and ye shall hold your peace.'*

"The battle is the Lord's. He has shown out and will continue to show out. That is just how He is!

"Look what the Lord did! He parted the Red Sea! The Jews will get across just fine. They are crossing over on dry ground! No getting stuck in the mud here. God always thinks of everything!

"I sure hope the Egyptians don't try and follow them. Oops, there they go. I'm guessing that many more than just Pharaoh will be leaving earth today. What a huge, eternal mistake they have made by not trusting and obeying the Lord.

"The fear of God should now be with the Israelites and all of the surrounding nations for generations to come. But why, oh why, do I get the feeling they will forget this down the road? That this will not be the last time God has to get their full and complete attention. They seem to be such a rebellious people. I hope they don't return to their old ways, but I am not betting the farm on it."

"Looks like God is doing some writing for Moses. He will probably write a whole book one day! Maybe even become the best-selling author in the history of the world! I will put my oats on that! Since He is writing, those people need to pay attention and read well. When the finger of God moves, they better perk up and listen to what He says," Ivory told his friends.

THE TEN COMMANDMENTS

I am the LORD thy God, which have brought thee out of the land of Egypt, out of the house of bondage.

Thou shalt have no other gods before me.

Thou shalt not make unto thee any graven image, or any likeness of any thing that is in heaven above, or that is in the earth beneath, or that is in the water under the earth.

Thou shalt not bow down thyself to them, nor serve them: for I the LORD thy God am a jealous God, visiting the iniquity of the fathers upon the children unto the third and fourth generation of them that hate me;

And shewing mercy unto thousands of them that love me, and keep my commandments.

Thou shalt not take the name of the LORD thy God in vain; for the LORD will not hold him guiltless that taketh his name in vain.

Remember the sabbath day, to keep it holy.

Six days shalt thou labour, and do all thy work:

But the seventh day is the sabbath of the LORD thy God: in it thou shalt not do any work, thou, nor thy son, nor thy daughter, thy manservant, nor thy maidservant, nor thy cattle, nor thy stranger that is within thy gates:

For in six days the LORD made heaven and earth, the sea, and all that in them is, and rested the seventh day: wherefore the LORD blessed the sabbath day, and hallowed it.

Honour thy father and thy mother: that thy days may be long upon the land which the LORD thy God giveth thee.

Thou shalt not kill.

Thou shalt not commit adultery.

Thou shalt not steal.

Thou shalt not bear false witness against thy neighbour.

Thou shalt not covet thy neighbour's house, thou shalt not covet thy neighbour's wife, nor his manservant, nor his maidservant, nor his ox, nor his ass, nor any thing that is thy neighbour's.

"One thing about horses is they love to run free. They really don't like boundaries or to be corralled. Many breeds can be domesticated, but their nature is freedom. They have a fight-or-flight syndrome. When horses are threatened, many times they will flee; but at other times, they will stay, fight, and protect their offspring. But horses have boundaries, as well. Their age is a boundary. Oceans they cannot cross are a boundary. Strength can be a boundary when compared to other horses, too.

"It doesn't end there. Within a herd of horses, there is a hierarchy: a pecking order. It is natural for horses to test their boundaries and test where they are in the pecking order when they want to move up. There is also security in knowing where they are in that pecking order.

"We watch humans do the same thing. They test the boundaries of relationships, work rules, and other areas around them. Danger comes when they test the boundaries God has laid out for them. When they live within His boundaries, there is literal joy in their lives. When they step outside the boundaries of the commandments He has laid down, there is unspeakable trouble. They have no clue what awaits them. They seem like wild horses that have a wild heart. They sure seem like unbreakable horses at times.

"Those commandments are so simple, yet so profound. Pure truth from the hands of Almighty God. Not too hard to keep them. Common sense. Straightforward. Easily for the betterment of all people and all societies on planet Earth. I guess I am wondering how long it will take them to break those commandments! My guess is it will happen rather quickly. It looks to me like they need some good old horse sense. They have accumulated a lot of knowledge in life, but it doesn't seem to have done many of them much good. I think they are going to break those commandments. I also think, probably, many of them already know that deep down. Maybe that is the point. They can't keep them, so they need to keep coming to Him and Him alone to seek forgiveness. It will be fascinating to watch how all of this plays out. All I know is if God gives some lasting words to His people, they should read and heed anything He has to say."

"Since forgetting God seems to be a national pastime for the Jews, it looks like He is giving them certain days and feasts to celebrate Him and keep them very close to Him. That is really a fascinating idea. Those folks down there have the tendency to wander off, but these feasts will always remind them to keep their attention on their Creator. I guess, since we can see Him, it is much easier for us to keep our focus. They can't see Him, but they know He is there. They know the wonderful creation they live in just screams, as loud as loud can be, that there is an amazing Creator who put it all together," Elap shared with the others.

"Do you see how He is giving them one day a week for the Sabbath? It is just like when He created everything! He worked for six days and then rested on the seventh. He was giving them an example! We always know there is purpose to whatever He does. The Sabbath is a day of rest and a day to draw closer to the Lord. A day that reminds them of His great creative ability and a day that keeps their focus in the right place.

"Passover is a wonderful feast of the Lord. Remember when Moses and the great Exodus were happening and God, once again, decided to save His people? He had them sacrifice a lamb and place the blood of that lamb over their doorposts. God was going to smite the firstborn of both man and beast; but if He saw the blood on the door posts, He would *pass over* that home. God is reminding them of His grace and His mercy to all people. Passover will be a lasting memorial of the Most High God delivering them from their slavery in Egypt.

"Now He is giving them the Feast of Unleavened Bread. There can be no yeast in the bread they partake of. Seems simple to me why this is one of their feasts. It is a reminder of their very hasty exit from Egypt; and also, that yeast is always a symbol of sin, evil, and false doctrine. God wants His people to walk a holy walk. He wants them to walk—no run—away from sin in their lives. This is a reminder of how sin can affect someone's entire life, just like yeast can affect an entire batch of dough.

"On the Feast of First Fruits, the Israelites are to wave a sheaf of grain before the Lord to remind them of the fertile land He has given them. This spring feast is meant to be a time of thanks for the crops and food the Lord has, one more time, provided for them. It celebrates the harvest. They never want to forget how generous the Lord has been with them.

"Fifty days later, they are supposed to celebrate the great Feast of Pentecost by waving two loaves of bread before the Lord. This is the day God came down to Mt. Sinai in a cloud with fire and gave the Law to Moses. It was one of the most amazing experiences we have ever seen.

"In the fall, there are other feasts. Rosh Hashanah, also known as the Feast of Trumpets, starts off the Jewish new year. The blowing of the ram's horn, or shofar, is always a joyous time to the Lord. There is something about those trumpet sounds that brings joy to His ears. These trumpet blasts are the beginning of the high holy days or, as some say, the Days of Awe. This is really a time of repentance, and always will be, even as the times become more serious.

"Ten days after Rosh Hashanah is Yom Kippur, or the Day of Atonement. This is considered by many to be the highest of all holy days. This is such a solemn feast. There is no eating or drinking on this day. No work at all can be done. Sins need to be confessed and atoned for from the previous year. Nothing else matters. Being right with the Lord is the only focus.

"And the last of these major feast days is the Feast of Tabernacles. This is also called the Feast of Booths. Five days after the Day of Atonement, they are to build booths to live in for seven days. God has so graciously provided shelter for them throughout their lives. It is a joyous time of celebration. It is a thankful time of remembering the Most High God. It is a grand time of rejoicing!"

"What an incredible time that was for Israel! God said He would gain glory for His Name by delivering them from the bondage of Egypt; and boy, did He ever! From that time on, the whole world knew that the God of Israel is the true God," Crimson recalled.

"And their deliverance led them straight to the truth of the Law and the celebrations of God. No other people on earth had those kinds of privileges! Profound, if you ask me," Ivory remarked as they moved along.

"And it didn't stop there," Elap added as he watched his step.

"You mean when He actually came down from Heaven and met with men?" Ivory filled in.

"Exactly," Elap agreed. *"If they didn't meet with Him in faith, they met Him in disobedience, and some of them were in for some big surprises!"*

Chapter 5
You Haven't Seen the Last of Him

"*I guess one of the* most obvious things we can figure out is how much Jesus loves the people He created. I can't read His mind, but I bet He thinks about them constantly. I get the feeling He is concerned about them all of the time," Onyx concluded.

"Why do you think that way?" Crimson wondered.

"Look at Him. It's like He wants to be with them as much as possible. He goes down there and visits them so much.

"You remember when He was walking in the cool of the Garden with Adam and Eve. Everything was perfect back then. He wanted to spend so much time with them. But, of course, they chose to sin, which always breaks fellowship with the Lord.

"When He appeared to Abraham in the plains of Mamre, it was a beautiful time. He just sat with Abraham at the doorway of his tent during the heat of the day. We could see how much He enjoyed being there.

"We also know how much He loves Jacob! You remember when He got into that wrestling match with him. Now we knew there was no way Jesus would lose, but I'm not sure Jacob realized that! They wrestled the whole night, and, of course, Jacob wanted a blessing. Who wouldn't want a blessing from the Lord Himself?! He changed Jacob's name to *Israel,* which means 'a prince with God,' and he would have favor with God and men. Jacob was never the same after his encounter with Jesus, and no one should ever be the same after encountering Him either!

"Y'all remember when the Lord was the pillar of fire that sheltered the camp of Israel as they left Egypt? Jesus was protecting them, and nothing could harm them. He has always had that loving, fatherly-protecting quality to Him, but I am not sure the people down there realize that side of Him.

"Jesus' love for Balaam was so great that He even stopped his donkey one time! Balaam couldn't see Jesus, but his donkey could. And that donkey was going to obey the Lord! We love it when those from the equine family know their place and know to always obey the King of Kings!

"Of course, none of us liked when Balaam kept striking his donkey. Balaam couldn't see. He couldn't see what was going on around him. He was walking by sight and not by faith. Jesus was in control. Jesus was protecting him, and he didn't even know it.

"Then Jesus opened his eyes, and Balaam could see Him! Balaam knew immediately that he had sinned. When he saw His holiness, he knew he was out of line. It was that apparent and that quick. Jesus was protecting him. Jesus always—and I do mean always—has every person's best interests at heart. I really wish more people would recognize that.

"God is always about getting people's attention. What they don't realize is that they always have His attention. He must think about them all the time. But they are so quick to turn away. They can so easily wander off the narrow path that He has set before them. Then when they wind up in trouble, they typically want to blame Him. Makes no sense. But then again, we can't see it from their angle, and they can't see it from ours.

"The Lord sure does love Joshua. How much more could He have expressed it when He met Joshua that time by Jericho? Joshua was a strong and courageous man of God. When he looked up and saw the Lord standing there, Joshua asked if He was for them or for their adversaries. Now I know Joshua had to ask that question; but from up here and from Jesus' perspective, there was absolutely no reason to ask! Jesus is always for His people. He is always their Protector and Comforter! He will always take care of them, even in the seemingly most dire of circumstances. He will increase their faith, it seems, whether they like it or not.

"Then Joshua fell down to worship Him as the Captain of the Lord's host. People need to understand there is no worshiping anything or anyone other than God, and Joshua did just that. He fell on his face before the Lord, who stood before him with drawn sword to lead the armies of Israel to victory against their adversaries. Since everything was created by Jesus, nothing in creation even comes close to who He is. Only *One* gets the glory at any time, including the credit for the exploits of Joshua. He—and He alone—is the Commander-In-Chief.

"We can tell how much the Lord loves Gideon! He is God's kind of man. The Jews always seem to get off the path and worship other gods. They should know that after God saved them out of Egypt, they should never—and I do mean never—fear any other god. Never. The God whom they worship is the only God! There is none other. He is the everlasting One. I just can't believe how quickly their eyes can start looking in a different direction.

"Jesus reminded Gideon that He would use him to save the Jewish people and be with him every step of the way. *Gideon, you can trust Me* seems to be what He wanted Gideon to know. If only all of those people down there would realize that, too, then life would be so much simpler and better for them.

"I love Daniel. What a man of God. No backing up with him. He will serve God and live, or serve God and die. No middle ground with him. Take it or leave it. He just didn't care what the people of the world thought of him. He is a God pleaser and not a man pleaser. I wish more people could see how important it is to live their lives this way. God will either protect them or allow them to give up the ghost and come be with Him! Either way, God is going to be glorified. Bring glory to the One who deserves glory. Bring honor to the One who deserves honor. Bring worship to the One who deserves worship. Nothing else really matters. They need to think about that.

"Daniel is such a great leader, and he and his friends will not be bowing down to a statue. They will not be bowing down to false gods. They aren't wired that way as servants of the Most High God. They have that look of steel. They are strong like flint. They are as strong and solid as Stone Mountain. No moving them.

"So, of course, they get in trouble with King Nebuchadnezzar! Followers of the Lord may seem to cause trouble in the world's eyes, but they are by no means in trouble in the Lord's eyes. It is all about perspective.

"Nebuchadnezzar has decided to throw Shadrach, Meshach, and Abednego into the fiery furnace. Of course, that means certain death for them unless the Lord steps in. And that, He does! When Nebuchadnezzar looked and saw four men in that furnace, one of them looked like the Son of God! Well, there was a reason for that. He was! The faith and trust that these men and all followers of Jesus have is really astonishing. We can see Him, and have seen Him, for a long time. They haven't seen Him yet. They just have to trust Him, and the ones who do—wow, does God always do something mighty in their lives!

"The Lord goes there and visits so often. We get the feeling He might just want to go and stay awhile! Boy, He sure does love those folks down there.

"We know this won't be the last time they see Him. And it can be good or bad when they have their next encounter with Him."

As they continued walking along, Onyx recalled, "Wasn't it great to see how the Lord responded to the faith of those men by delivering them from impossible circumstances?"

"Yes, and He wasn't about to let people forget about those miraculous deeds He performed either. He wanted a written record of what He had done, and what He intended to do, for them in the future!" Crimson explained.

"And as we watched it being written, we knew God wasn't done blowing their hooves off! Could you believe all the things He tucked into that record He gave them? Amazing!" Onyx added.

Chapter 6
Write Down to the Last Detail

"**Of there is one thing** we know about the Jewish people, it is their love for the Word of God. They know it is essential to their existence. They know that God Himself has entrusted them with His words. This is no laughing matter. This is very serious business. They realize, like we do, that Satan would want to destroy God's Word. God is giving the world His commands. He is giving them His instructions. He is giving them His love," Ivory expounded.

"So, of course, the one book that Satan would love to corrupt is the canon of Scripture. God wants to use these writings to reveal Himself to all mankind and to show how much He loves them. He gave mankind the ability to read, and they are supposed to read His most blessed Word. This is why the Jews take so, so seriously how they treat the Word of God. They know these are not their words, but God's. They also know they have the huge, eternal responsibility to make sure the next generation coming after them has these words in the exact fashion as they did. No changes. No mistakes. No errors. God doesn't change, God doesn't make mistakes, and God has no errors. So if the next generation is going to understand the One True God, His words must be correctly preserved for all of the generations in the future.

"The tribe of Levi had the massive privilege of protecting the words of God. As we know, they were more than up to the task. They needed to be fervent and passionate about the Holy Scriptures, and they were.

"Any of those folks down there can make a mistake when they copy something. My goodness, if they made the mistake in the Garden of eating from the *only* tree God said not to eat from, they could certainly mess this up, as well! But the Most High God always has a remnant in every generation who takes Him seriously and takes Him at His word. Pun intended!

"Copies of the Scriptures were made on animal skins or papyrus, which would wear out over time. So what would happen to God's Word? It needed to be copied, and it needed to be copied correctly!

"To make sure there were no blunders or missteps, rules were put into place. Some of those rules really are fascinating. When it came time to write God's Name, the scribes had to wash their hands, use a special brush or pen that was used for that Name and that Name only, and then wash their hands again! Now that is dedication. They loved God so much and knew He is a holy God. They realized this was not something to mess around with. This was very serious business.

"They also had to have the same total of words on each copy as they compared it to the original. It had to have the same number of lines and the same amount of words on each line when compared to the original. Copies were always verified and checked by other scribes. The middle letter of the original document had to be the middle letter on the copy, which was another thing they looked for. What if they messed up? What if there was a mistake? That is what fire is for! They had to feed that fire to keep it going. Any copies with even the slightest mistake made it into the fire. They couldn't take the chance that a flawed copy would ever get into circulation. Not only would it make them look bad, but it would make God look bad. No way on earth would they ever make God look bad.

"Now another interesting thing is that the scribes thought the newer copy was actually more accurate than the older one! They were so meticulous in their work that they knew there would be no issues at all with the copy they made. But that produced a dilemma: What should they do with the older copies? What they did was put them in clay jars and bury them. That would preserve them. They couldn't burn those because they were the accurate words of God. They had no right—and no one has any right—to destroy God's literal words. That is why people down there will probably, one day, find some of these clay jars; and when they look inside, they will find out exactly how accurate the scribes have been throughout the years!

"The Word of God is so special that a copy was always kept in the Ark of the Covenant. It was like a master copy. The prophet Ezra's love for the Lord was paramount. He was used by God to put all of the books of the Old Testament together. He loved the Holy Scriptures and wanted other people to love them and study them, as well. He challenged many to do just that. Ezra was a teacher at heart. He wanted the Jews to be a consecrated people who stopped living like the world. He knew that if they loved the Word of God, obeyed it, and washed their minds in it, they had a great chance at living like the obedient followers and remnant believers did in the generations before them. And that has me thinking. There is something fascinating in those scrolls making my wheels spin. It is like a puzzle, and I'm beginning to figure it out.

"All right now, this is interesting. As I have been looking over their shoulders all of these years and watching them copy those texts, I've noticed that they seem to be telling us history in advance, kind of like foretelling the future. Now, we all know that God is all-knowing. There is nothing He does not know. Nothing catches Him off guard—and I do mean nothing. These prophecies are like breadcrumbs leading to something. They are like pieces of a puzzle that are right before people's eyes; and all they have to do is look and turn to God, and they could fit them all together. Basically, it is really that simple.

"So let's see if we can figure this out. We are detectives now, and so let's look at the evidence in God's Word and see if we can identify who it says the Messiah will be.

"The clues tell us He will be born of a woman, so we know He will have a human side to Him. They also tell us He will come from the lineage of Abraham, Isaac, Jacob, and Judah. He will also come through the line of King David. That definitely narrows it down and eliminates people who are not of this bloodline.

"But now we have a dilemma. Isaiah—man, I love that guy— tells us that the Messiah will be born of a virgin. How can that happen? It takes a man and a woman to produce a child down there. That is obvious. So how can a virgin give birth to a child? This is getting more intriguing by the minute. We know it will come true because God has said it would. He never, ever breaks His Word. It is unfathomable to Him for something like that to happen. He has said it, so it will happen. Literally, that simple. Let's keep up the search and see where this goes.

"The Scriptures say the Messiah will be born in the small town of Bethlehem. There are a plethora of towns in Israel where someone can be born, but God has chosen this small town to bring the Messiah to the people of the world.

"A certain lineage, born of a virgin, and the town of Bethlehem. The pieces of the puzzle are coming together. Going to be interesting to see who this Messiah will be!"

"It is important to follow the evidence. For some who dwell on the earth, it might be their last chance to figure out who He really is," Onyx remarked.

"Amazing to see all that God had embedded in His Word!" Ivory halted to say.

"Even though He had given them so much, He was about to give them so, so much more!" Onyx also stopped to say.

"God told them exactly who to look for; and when those prophecies began to be fulfilled, the heavenlies just erupted in praise!" Ivory said, but added, "Let's not stop. We need to keep going."

Chapter 7
At Long, Long Last

"*Hey, fellas, look!*" *Flap said,* tossing his head. "He is leaving us again, but something is different. You can just tell. He will always be here since He is omnipresent. That will never change. But He loves those people so much. Looks like He is going back there again. Something tells me that this time will be much, much different than His other visits.

"Did you guys see that?! He was just birthed out of that lady. No way. She is a virgin. How can that be?

"Do you remember when we were talking about all of those prophecies concerning the long-awaited Messiah for the Jews?"

"Of course," Crimson answered. "It will be fascinating to see how they all play out."

"Well, play out indeed! It is Jesus. *HE* is the Messiah! *HE* is the One! *HE* is the only One who can fulfill all of those prophecies. Being born of the virgin, of the lineage of Judah, in the town of Bethlehem just solidifies everything. The probability of these prophecies coming true in anyone else is basically zilch, but the probability of these prophecies coming true in Jesus just hit 100%!!" Elap stated resoundingly.

"Wait. This begs the question: Why has He gone there? If He was born as a babe, does that mean He is going to stay down there awhile? Is He going to live a life like those humans do? Will He have to go through all the things they go through? Why would He do that? Why would He leave this gorgeous place? Why does He seem to love those people so much, when so many of them don't even give Him the time of day? This is a type of love that we just don't comprehend totally. Why, oh why?"

"You know what we need to do, don't you? We need to go back to the Holy Book to see what else it says. If it got everything right about His birth, then there must be other clues in there about His life, as well. Time to do some searching!" Crimson insisted.

"The Jewish Scriptures are so much fun to go through. They have so much truth in them that it is exciting to look over people's shoulders and read those words. To dig in and find those nuggets of truth.

"It says that many children are going to be killed at the time of Messiah's birth—a literal massacre of kids. That sounds just like the evil one, doesn't it? Murder is always the game he likes to play. He always wants to steal, kill, and destroy. He has wanted to destroy the works of God from the beginning. He will fail. We all know that. I sure hope those people down there come to realize that fact, too.

"Now this has me thinking. Those Scriptures say that Messiah will be called *Emmanuel*. We know that means 'God with us.' Isn't that the big, big clue? Isn't it the piece of information that should have told us God was going to visit His creation as their Messiah? We should have seen this One coming!

"They also say He will be declared the *'Son of God.'* As you can see, this is becoming so much clearer. All of the evidence is right there.

"The Scriptures say He will spend a season in Egypt. There will be a forerunner who announces His coming. The Scriptures let us know that the Messiah will be a Prophet—a Prophet like Moses—and He will be called a Nazarene.

"The Oracles of God tell us His own people will reject Him. Why is that not a surprise to us? We have already seen throughout history that the Jews and the people of earth seem to follow God for a while and then walk away from Him. Their eyes get a glimpse of something in the world, their direction changes, and they head right towards that worldly thing or event. So we should have figured that God would reach out to them one more time—or should we say for the one millionth time—and they would reject Him. They would not be interested. They think they are in control, so let's not mess up what we have going on down here. My goodness. What love the Lord has! What compassion the Lord has! What kindness the Lord has! What grace the Lord has! What mercy the Lord has! Why don't these people see this? How can they literally be so blind when God is shining the brightest laser beam of light revealing who He is right in their eyes?

"The prophecies continue to tell us that He will be praised by children, and He will speak in parables. All of this was envisioned by the prophets, so it will come true. When God speaks, it will come to pass. But there is something even more intriguing in all of these writings. They seem to be foretelling the death of the Messiah! Look at some of these Scriptures and what they say.

"The Scriptures tell us He will have a triumphal entry into Jerusalem. They say He will be betrayed. That is not surprising because it seems to be commonplace on earth to betray others and God. He will be falsely accused. The money He is betrayed for will be used to buy a potter's field. Money, money, money. Every time we look down there it seems like people are chasing money. It is just like chasing the wind. They get some money, and it flies away. It goes away so quickly. The crazy thing is that money brings so many of those people trouble; and yet, they want more of it! Why don't they realize that a simple life of living for and obeying God is a wonderful life? All I know is that whoever sells out the Messiah for money is going to have trouble because of that choice.

"Not only will the Messiah be falsely accused, He will be silent before His accusers. They will hate Him without cause. They will spit on Him, strike Him, mock Him, and ridicule Him.

"He will be pierced in His hands and feet. I'm not sure what that means, but I shudder just thinking of it. He will be given vinegar to drink and will die with criminals. Wow. He is nothing of the sort. He is the Son of God. He hates evil; and yet, He will die with criminals? Unthinkable!

"They will gamble for His garments. He will pray for His enemies. His side will be pierced, but none of His bones will be broken. He will be buried with the rich but will rise from the dead! That is not surprising. If there is one thing we know, you can't keep a great Man down! He will ascend to Heaven and be seated at the right hand of the Father. None of that is surprising either. But a couple of things have really intrigued me here. The Scriptures say He will be forsaken by God. I don't have a clue how that can happen. There is no way, but the Scriptures say it will happen, so it will, even though I don't understand how. Also, they say He will be the sacrifice for sin. This is compelling. Why does He need to do that? Man, we have so much to learn!

"Why don't these truths resonate with those folks down there? It is like He is trying to reverberate truth in their ears, but they have shut Him out. It is like they are trying to block all the sounds He is sending their way. That is not a good strategy for them to live by.

"We see that the Messiah's days on earth have now started, but from what the Good Book says, He is going to have some last days down there, as well."

 "Didn't we know something big was going on when the scribes recorded the Word of God?" Elap marveled as he walked along.

"Yes, but we weren't quite sure how it would all play out," Crimson answered.

"God definitely had a last trump card to play against the devil and sin, and play it He did. Seeing the prophecies about Messiah come true was exhilarating, yet difficult to watch," Elap said and then added, "Let's make sure to keep moving, fellas."

Chapter 8
The First and The Last

"**W***atching Jesus grow up is* fascinating. He is 100% God; and yet, 100% man at the same time. This is really captivating," Onyx observed.

"*'And Jesus increased in wisdom and stature, and in favour with God and man.'* That is so true. His knowledge is out of this world; but, of course, we already knew that! He is growing physically since He is in a human body. So He will continue to grow like other men do. God will give Him favor for sure. He loves Him so very, very much! It is hard to put their relationship into words. There is a plan going on here that will be exciting to see how it all concludes!

"Hey, look. Jesus is being baptized in the Jordan River. That is intriguing. We can already tell that this is the start of something special!

"The Holy Spirit just landed on Him like a dove!

"God has just spoken and said, *'This is my beloved Son, in whom I am well pleased.'* You better believe He is pleased with Him! He is pleased with Him today, tomorrow, and for all of eternity! Something big is going on here, and it seems like it is just the beginning. Not sure what it might be, but we better keep our eyes open because something exceptional is about to occur."

"Here comes the enemy again," Crimson interjected. "He is going to tempt Jesus? He must be kidding. It will never work.

"Well, Jesus did just fast for forty days and forty nights so Satan must think there is a slim chance he can get Him to fall for one of his dastardly tricks. From the view we have up here, that just isn't going to work!

"'*Command that these stones be made bread*'? Is he kidding me? He created the whole world! The whole universe! The whole shooting match! He can create anything He wants to. Jesus just responded with, '*It is written, Man shall not live by bread alone, but by every word that proceedeth out of the mouth of God.*'

"Now that was a nice comeback! What is more important than a morsel of bread? A buffet of God's words!

"So Satan is trying to convince Jesus to throw Himself off the pinnacle of the Temple? I don't think so! That won't be happening. Just like before, Jesus' response is perfect, '*It is written again, Thou shalt not tempt the Lord thy God.*'

"You would think the evil one would learn. You would think he would realize that tempting the Creator of the universe will never work, but he is a pesky one. He does have perseverance, even though he will end up with a zero percent success rate against the King of Kings.

"Satan is telling Jesus that if He bows down and worships him, he will give Him all of the kingdoms of the world? This snake is clueless. Did you hear that? Jesus just said, '*Get thee hence, Satan: for it is written, Thou shalt worship the Lord thy God, and him only shalt thou serve.*'

"That is zero for three where I come from. That is a very bad strikeout. But do you see what Jesus is doing? He is giving people a lesson here. I hope they get it."

"What do you mean?" Onyx inquired.

"Every time Satan tempted Jesus, how did He respond? He said, '*It is written,*' and then He would quote the Word of God. He just quoted the book of Deuteronomy three times. He is showing the importance of the Torah. He is showing them that when temptations and battles come from the archenemy of God, go right to the Scriptures. Go to eternal truth. Go to what works every time. If the Word was good enough for Jesus to use when He was tempted, it is good enough for those folks who are traversing across that beautiful blue planet, too. Will they learn? Will they see the Master's plan? Will they follow His plan? Only time will tell.

"Hey, look. He just did His first miracle down there!

"We just know those folks will question it and try to explain it away, but I'm not sure how they will do that! Even we can see He is working His wonders once again!

"He is trying to show them, once more, that He is the Creator of all and over all. He is taking nothing and making something from it again. Water. H_2O. And then He turns it into wine? There is nothing in water that makes it wine. Only His hands could do something like that. His grand and immortal fingerprints are on everything surrounding those folks. Why won't they dust for them and discern His handiwork in all that's going on around them?

"He had power over the elements at creation, and He still does today. But we know what He is doing. He is showing them His divine nature. They will, no doubt, question it and have issues with it, so He is giving them the evidence they need to make their decision. The ones who do will strengthen their faith immensely in the days to come.

"It looks like He is about to speak to a big group of folks down there. He is going up on the mount to talk with them from there. Since He is about to teach, we had better listen in on this."

THE SERMON ON THE MOUNT

Blessed are the poor in spirit: for theirs is the kingdom of heaven.

Blessed are they that mourn: for they shall be comforted.

Blessed are the meek: for they shall inherit the earth.

Blessed are they which do hunger and thirst after righteousness: for they shall be filled.

Blessed are the merciful: for they shall obtain mercy.

Blessed are the pure in heart: for they shall see God.

Blessed are the peacemakers: for they shall be called the children of God.

Blessed are they which are persecuted for righteousness' sake: for theirs is the kingdom of heaven.

Blessed are ye, when men shall revile you, and persecute you, and shall say all manner of evil against you falsely, for my sake.

Rejoice, and be exceeding glad: for great is your reward in heaven: for so persecuted they the prophets which were before you.

Ye are the salt of the earth: but if the salt have lost his savour, wherewith shall it be salted? it is thenceforth good for nothing, but to be cast out, and to be trodden under foot of men.

Ye are the light of the world. A city that is set on an hill cannot be hid.

Neither do men light a candle, and put it under a bushel, but on a candlestick; and it giveth light unto all that are in the house.

Let your light so shine before men, that they may see your good works, and glorify your Father which is in heaven.

Think not that I am come to destroy the law, or the prophets: I am not come to destroy, but to fulfil.

For verily I say unto you, Till heaven and earth pass, one jot or one tittle shall in no wise pass from the law, till all be fulfilled.

Whosoever therefore shall break one of these least commandments, and shall teach men so, he shall be called the least in the kingdom of heaven: but whosoever shall do and teach them, the same shall be called great in the kingdom of heaven.

For I say unto you, That except your righteousness shall exceed the righteousness of the scribes and Pharisees, ye shall in no case enter into the kingdom of heaven.

Ye have heard that it was said of them of old time, Thou shalt not kill; and whosoever shall kill shall be in danger of the judgment:

But I say unto you, That whosoever is angry with his brother without a cause shall be in danger of the judgment: and whosoever shall say to his brother, Raca, shall be in danger of the council: but whosoever shall say, Thou fool, shall be in danger of hell fire.

Therefore if thou bring thy gift to the altar, and there rememberest that thy brother hath ought against thee;

Leave there thy gift before the altar, and go thy way; first be reconciled to thy brother, and then come and offer thy gift.

Agree with thine adversary quickly, whiles thou art in the way with him; lest at any time the adversary deliver thee to the judge, and the judge deliver thee to the officer, and thou be cast into prison.

Verily I say unto thee, Thou shalt by no means come out thence, till thou hast paid the uttermost farthing.

Ye have heard that it was said by them of old time, Thou shalt not commit adultery:

But I say unto you, That whosoever looketh on a woman to lust after her hath committed adultery with her already in his heart.

And if thy right eye offend thee, pluck it out, and cast it from thee: for it is profitable for thee that one of thy members should perish, and not that thy whole body should be cast into hell.

And if thy right hand offend thee, cut it off, and cast it from thee: for it is profitable for thee that one of thy members should perish, and not that thy whole body should be cast into hell.

It hath been said, Whosoever shall put away his wife, let him give her a writing of divorcement:

But I say unto you, That whosoever shall put away his wife, saving for the cause of fornication, causeth her to commit adultery: and whosoever shall marry her that is divorced committeth adultery.

Again, ye have heard that it hath been said by them of old time, Thou shalt not forswear thyself, but shalt perform unto the Lord thine oaths:

But I say unto you, Swear not at all; neither by heaven; for it is God's throne:

Nor by the earth; for it is his footstool: neither by Jerusalem; for it is the city of the great King.

Neither shalt thou swear by thy head, because thou canst not make one hair white or black.

But let your communication be, Yea, yea; Nay, nay: for whatsoever is more than these cometh of evil.

Ye have heard that it hath been said, An eye for an eye, and a tooth for a tooth:

But I say unto you, That ye resist not evil: but whosoever shall smite thee on thy right cheek, turn to him the other also.

And if any man will sue thee at the law, and take away thy coat, let him have thy cloak also.

And whosoever shall compel thee to go a mile, go with him twain.

Give to him that asketh thee, and from him that would borrow of thee turn not thou away.

Ye have heard that it hath been said, Thou shalt love thy neighbour, and hate thine enemy.

But I say unto you, Love your enemies, bless them that curse you, do good to them that hate you, and pray for them which despitefully use you, and persecute you;

That ye may be the children of your Father which is in heaven: for he maketh his sun to rise on the evil and on the good, and sendeth rain on the just and on the unjust.

For if ye love them which love you, what reward have ye? do not even the publicans the same?

And if ye salute your brethren only, what do ye more than others? do not even the publicans so?

Be ye therefore perfect, even as your Father which is in heaven is perfect.

Take heed that ye do not your alms before men, to be seen of them: otherwise ye have no reward of your Father which is in heaven.

Therefore when thou doest thine alms, do not sound a trumpet before thee, as the hypocrites do in the synagogues and in the streets, that they may have glory of men. Verily I say unto you, They have their reward.

But when thou doest alms, let not thy left hand know what thy right hand doeth:

That thine alms may be in secret: and thy Father which seeth in secret himself shall reward thee openly.

And when thou prayest, thou shalt not be as the hypocrites are: for they love to pray standing in the synagogues and in the corners of the streets, that they may be seen of men. Verily I say unto you, They have their reward.

But thou, when thou prayest, enter into thy closet, and when thou hast shut thy door, pray to thy Father which is in secret; and thy Father which seeth in secret shall reward thee openly.

But when ye pray, use not vain repetitions, as the heathen do: for they think that they shall be heard for their much speaking.

Be not ye therefore like unto them: for your Father knoweth what things ye have need of, before ye ask him.

After this manner therefore pray ye: Our Father which art in heaven, Hallowed be thy name.

Thy kingdom come, Thy will be done in earth, as it is in heaven.

Give us this day our daily bread.

And forgive us our debts, as we forgive our debtors.

And lead us not into temptation, but deliver us from evil: For thine is the kingdom, and the power, and the glory, for ever. Amen.

For if ye forgive men their trespasses, your heavenly Father will also forgive you:

But if ye forgive not men their trespasses, neither will your Father forgive your trespasses.

Moreover when ye fast, be not, as the hypocrites, of a sad countenance: for they disfigure their faces, that they may appear unto men to fast. Verily I say unto you, They have their reward.

But thou, when thou fastest, anoint thine head, and wash thy face;

That thou appear not unto men to fast, but unto thy Father which is in secret: and thy Father, which seeth in secret, shall reward thee openly.

Lay not up for yourselves treasures upon earth, where moth and rust doth corrupt, and where thieves break through and steal:

But lay up for yourselves treasures in heaven, where neither moth nor rust doth corrupt, and where thieves do not break through nor steal:

For where your treasure is, there will your heart be also.

The light of the body is the eye: if therefore thine eye be single, thy whole body shall be full of light.

But if thine eye be evil, thy whole body shall be full of darkness. If therefore the light that is in thee be darkness, how great is that darkness!

No man can serve two masters: for either he will hate the one, and love the other; or else he will hold to the one, and despise the other. Ye cannot serve God and mammon.

Therefore I say unto you, Take no thought for your life, what ye shall eat, or what ye shall drink; nor yet for your body, what ye shall put on. Is not the life more than meat, and the body than raiment?

Behold the fowls of the air: for they sow not, neither do they reap, nor gather into barns; yet your heavenly Father feedeth them. Are ye not much better than they?

Which of you by taking thought can add one cubit unto his stature?

And why take ye thought for raiment? Consider the lilies of the field, how they grow; they toil not, neither do they spin:

And yet I say unto you, That even Solomon in all his glory was not arrayed like one of these.

Wherefore, if God so clothe the grass of the field, which to day is, and to morrow is cast into the oven, shall he not much more clothe you, O ye of little faith?

Therefore take no thought, saying, What shall we eat? or, What shall we drink? or, Wherewithal shall we be clothed?

(For after all these things do the Gentiles seek:) for your heavenly Father knoweth that ye have need of all these things.

But seek ye first the kingdom of God, and his righteousness; and all these things shall be added unto you.

Take therefore no thought for the morrow: for the morrow shall take thought for the things of itself. Sufficient unto the day is the evil thereof.

Judge not, that ye be not judged.

For with what judgment ye judge, ye shall be judged: and with what measure ye mete, it shall be measured to you again.

And why beholdest thou the mote that is in thy brother's eye, but considerest not the beam that is in thine own eye?

Or how wilt thou say to thy brother, Let me pull out the mote out of thine eye; and, behold, a beam is in thine own eye?

Thou hypocrite, first cast out the beam out of thine own eye; and then shalt thou see clearly to cast out the mote out of thy brother's eye.

Give not that which is holy unto the dogs, neither cast ye your pearls before swine, lest they trample them under their feet, and turn again and rend you.

Ask, and it shall be given you; seek, and ye shall find; knock, and it shall be opened unto you:

For every one that asketh receiveth; and he that seeketh

findeth; and to him that knocketh it shall be opened.

Or what man is there of you, whom if his son ask bread, will he give him a stone?

Or if he ask a fish, will he give him a serpent?

If ye then, being evil, know how to give good gifts unto your children, how much more shall your Father which is in heaven give good things to them that ask him?

Therefore all things whatsoever ye would that men should do to you, do ye even so to them: for this is the law and the prophets.

Enter ye in at the strait gate: for wide is the gate, and broad is the way, that leadeth to destruction, and many there be which go in thereat:

Because strait is the gate, and narrow is the way, which leadeth unto life, and few there be that find it.

Beware of false prophets, which come to you in sheep's clothing, but inwardly they are ravening wolves.

Ye shall know them by their fruits. Do men gather grapes of thorns, or figs of thistles?

Even so every good tree bringeth forth good fruit; but a corrupt tree bringeth forth evil fruit.

A good tree cannot bring forth evil fruit, neither can a corrupt tree bring forth good fruit.

Every tree that bringeth not forth good fruit is hewn down, and cast into the fire.

Wherefore by their fruits ye shall know them.

Not every one that saith unto me, Lord, Lord, shall enter into the kingdom of heaven; but he that doeth the will of my Father which is in heaven.

Many will say to me in that day, Lord, Lord, have we not prophesied in thy name? and in thy name have cast out devils? and in thy name done many wonderful works?

And then will I profess unto them, I never knew you: depart from me, ye that work iniquity.

Therefore whosoever heareth these sayings of mine, and doeth them, I will liken him unto a wise man, which built his house upon a rock.

And the rain descended, and the floods came, and the winds blew, and beat upon that house; and it fell not: for it was founded upon a rock.

And every one that heareth these sayings of mine, and doeth them not, shall be likened

> unto a foolish man, which built his house upon the sand:
>
> And the rain descended, and the floods came, and the winds blew, and beat upon that house; and it fell: and great was the fall of it.
>
> And it came to pass, when Jesus had ended these sayings, the people were astonished at his doctrine:
>
> For he taught them as one having authority, and not as the scribes.

"We know how much He loves them. We know it throughout our entire beings. Do they get it, though? Are they going to run to Him, or run away from Him? Do they have any clue how much wisdom was just placed in front of them? Will they dissect it and digest it and make it part of their lives? Or, will they go to lunch now and forget about, probably, the greatest sermon their ears will ever hear in their lifetimes? I sure wish they could see from our perspective how important that message is," Crimson concluded.

"Not only does Jesus love to do miracles, He knows they glorify His Father in Heaven. Look down there. It's predicament time again for those folks! Five loaves and two fish to feed around 20,000 people, including the women and children.

"Do you see the looks on their faces? It's like, *No way, José,* is that going to cut it. Another hungry night on planet Earth. What they don't realize is a little in the hand of God can turn into a lot. This is going to be exciting!

"Amazing what He just did! He turned that minuscule amount of food into a bountiful harvest! Not only did all the people sit down and rest in the Lord, but the King who controls all of those elements just shocked the house again! Everyone was fed, and twelve basketfuls were left over! They knew they didn't have enough to eat, but they turned to the Son of God and wound up with a buffet!"

"Now the thought-provoking thing is this: Will they pay attention to what just happened? Will they forget it two seconds later? Will they remember it when the hunger pangs set back in soon? Will this miracle of the fishes and loaves come back to them when they are on the high seas of trouble in their lives? Will they remember Whom they need to cry out to?" Onyx interceded.

"That lot of people down there seems pretty forgetful. They remember God one moment and so easily turn their eyes away from Him the next. The days ahead for them are going to be very challenging if they don't stay focused on Jesus."

"What are those prophets doing down there?! Why are Elijah and Moses appearing with Jesus?" Onyx blared.

"Well, you know He is trying to teach them something. He always is!" Crimson replied.

"We don't even need to describe Jesus being transfigured on the mount. We have seen that glory up here and know what it is like, but those folks are going to be messed up in the head trying to figure it out!

"Since Moses and Elijah represent so much, their appearing shows them that Jesus has fulfilled the Law and the Prophets. Jesus is also showing them that He is way, way, way above any of the previous prophets.

"God has just spoken from Heaven saying, *'This is my beloved Son, in whom I am well pleased; hear ye him.'* Pretty simple, isn't it? Hear Him. Listen to Him. Obey Him. If folks would just keep it simple. Instead, they muddy it up with their pride, or they let Satan come in and have his way. If they would just keep it simple, they would get so much more done for the Lord.

"Did you see what Jesus just did? When the disciples fell on their faces after hearing the voice of God, they were greatly afraid. We could tell it caught them way off guard! So Jesus walked over to them. He reached down. He touched them and told them to rise and not be afraid. His grace and compassion are literally other-worldly. I hope those folks down there realize Whose presence they're in."

"Do you think those people totally understand how much the Lord loves them?" Onyx wondered.

"I am going to guess not, and I am going to make my guess based on empirical evidence. I have seen them, so many times, literally just walk away from Him. Their eyes have seen Him do amazing things all throughout history; and yet, just a short time afterward, they have ditched Him and are living for the world. So I am going to say 'no.'

"Do you see Jesus weeping? He loves Lazarus so much. When one of their good buds dies, it must be hard. There is no death up here, so we don't experience that sorrow.

"Everyone seems to be crying down there. Lazarus touched many, many lives during his time there. More men of God need to do the same before they take their last breath.

"Jesus just told the people that Lazarus is asleep, but they don't grasp what He is saying. Death seems so final for everyone down there. They don't realize that people basically go to sleep and then wake up on our side. Death is just the opening of the door to eternal life. They see finality, and we see beginning. We can tell they don't realize what He meant by *asleep*.

"Jesus also just told them that He is the Resurrection and the Life. He is telling them that He has control over life and death. That is who He is. It is not over until He says it is over. He is also letting them know that people will rise from the dead. They will either rise to everlasting contempt or to everlasting righteousness, but they are going to rise.

"To see the Master weeping reveals how human He is, yet so divine at the same time. If they haven't figured out by now how much He loves them, this should do the trick.

"What did He just say? *'Lazarus, come forth'*?!

"Look! He is alive! He is walking and talking! Jesus, one more time, has shown them His power! He did this so they may believe. This off-the-chart miracle was done so they would know He is the Giver of life. So they would leave behind their lives of disbelief and distrust and live lives of hope, conviction, and confidence in the Savior! Do you think they will do it?"

"Only time will tell," Crimson considered.

"It looks like Jesus is entering Jerusalem on a donkey. He is the King! Shouldn't He be riding on a chariot or something? People should be carrying Him into Jerusalem. I guess He is, once again, showing people His humbleness. That quality just bleeds out of Him, doesn't it? I still wonder why He is arriving on that donkey."

"Do you remember, Onyx, when the Prophet Zechariah wrote: *'Rejoice greatly, O daughter of Zion; shout, O daughter of Jerusalem: behold, thy King cometh unto thee: he is just, and having salvation; lowly, and riding upon an ass, and upon a colt the foal of an ass'*? Looks like this prophecy is coming true right before our very eyes!

"Do you see all the people accompanying Him? They are laying down their clothes and spreading out palm branches for the donkey to walk upon.

"Do you hear them saying, *'Hosanna to the son of David: Blessed is he that cometh in the name of the Lord; Hosanna in the highest'*?

"I think they finally get it! They are giving Him the praise and adoration He deserves as the Son of God! Hallelujah! Even after all of the rejection throughout the years, I really think this is going to finally end well.

"The good news is that those folks down there like to eat! We will never argue with that. It is nice to get your friends together for a good meal, so it is good to see Him doing that.

"Why did Jesus just say, *'Ye know that after two days is the feast of the passover, and the Son of man is betrayed to be crucified'*?

"We have a problem here. People have been turning against Him so often that betraying Him doesn't surprise us. But crucified? I don't think this is going to end well after all. I must be wrong because we know He is in charge, so we know it has to end well! Everything ends well with Him. They need to make sure they walk by faith and not by sight. I know it will all come together somehow. Let's keep watching and listening.

"That woman just poured perfume over His head. We know what that means. Many times, it's used to prepare people for burial. Looks like His journey to planet Earth might be coming to an end.

"Can you believe Judas just covenanted to sell the Son of God for thirty pieces of silver?" Crimson snorted.

"Actually, I can. Judas has been skimming money from their bag. That money was meant for the poor, but Judas must have thought he fit that definition. He is greedy, and he has been stealing for a while now," Onyx responded.

"You don't think Jesus knew that?" Crimson questioned.

"Of course, He knew that. But that speaks to His character again. He is loving. He is gracious. He is kind. He gives people time to repent. What a great God He is! He wanted Judas, by his own free will, to repent and believe. Judas had choices to make, and as we can see from up here, they have culminated in him literally selling his soul for thirty pieces of silver," Onyx continued.

"Everyone has a price. They will sell their lives for something. Their whole life will be lived to be a great athlete, to pursue the perfect man or perfect woman, or chase a measly dollar bill. I sure wish they could see it from this perspective. None of that means anything up here in this place. Judas should repent, believe, and obey Jesus. All people on earth should do the same.

"Well, if this is playing out the way it looks like it is, then this is going to be the Last Supper that Jesus will have.

"The Passover meal should be such a joyous time, but if this is His last meal down there, we know He will turn that mourning into dancing! *Great* is going to come out of this somehow and someway.

"Do you see what is taking place during their Passover meal together: *'And as they were eating, Jesus took bread, and blessed it, and brake it, and gave it to the disciples, and said, Take, eat; this is my body. And he took the cup, and gave thanks, and gave it to them, saying, Drink ye all of it; For this is my blood of the new testament, which is shed for many for the remission of sins'?"*

"Jesus often gathers with His disciples in the Garden of Gethsemane, but it seems like the gardens down there cause so much trouble. They are so beautiful. Their colors and the smells are heavenly, but so many bad events keep happening in them," Ivory noted.

"Do you see Jesus praying in this garden? He just loves to pray. What a connection He has to His Father! He is really trusting His Father: *'O my Father, if it be possible, let this cup pass from me: nevertheless not as I will, but as thou wilt.'*

"What can't Jesus handle? He can handle anything. He is God. We know that. Why does He want this cup to pass from Him?

"He is praying and asking again, *'O my Father, if this cup may not pass away from me, except I drink it, thy will be done.'*

"I still don't understand any of this, but look at His attitude. He is determined to do the will of His Father even if it means dying. I am getting the feeling that is where all of this is heading. Why don't those people down there realize that doing God's will is the most important thing they will ever accomplish during their earthly years? It sure seems simple to me."

"The Chief Priests are coming to arrest Jesus," Elap noticed. "Jesus already knew it since He is all-knowing, but He isn't stopping them. He could stop them, or He could call down 10,000 angels to put all of this to rest, but He chooses not to. He always has the bigger plan in mind. He always has what is best for the Father in mind. The depth of His love for all people literally cannot be completely comprehended down there.

"Jesus is telling Peter, *'Put up thy sword into the sheath: the cup which my Father hath given me, shall I not drink it?'*

"It is amazing how many people want to live by the sword. There are times for it, but this is not one of them. Many people think the sword will solve their problems; but often times, it only creates more of them. If this whole experiment of planet Earth doesn't end soon, it wouldn't surprise me to see religious fanatics thinking they are doing God a favor by killing people by the sword; and, of course, they will be wrong.

"I love Peter's zeal, though. He is standing for Jesus. He is not backing down. He is His friend. He will fight for Him.

"Where is everyone else, though? Where are all the people Jesus fed with the fishes and loaves? Why aren't the other disciples running to His aid? You would think they love Him as much as He loves them and would stand with Him right to the end.

"Love can be so fleeting with them. Here one moment and then gone. I also think they don't understand. They are scared and confused. They probably thought Jesus would bring a peaceful panacea to earth, but it looks like that won't be happening at this time."

"Why are people mocking Him? Why are they saying, *'Hail, King of the Jews!'*? You don't mock God. That is blasphemous! Don't they realize that?" Onyx shouted.

"Now they are spitting on Him and striking Him? Okay, these people are officially in the crazy category now. You don't do that to God. But this is their choice. It is their free will to treat Him like this. Wow, have they been deceived. They literally have no clue what they are really doing.

"Nailing Him to a cross is unthinkable! They should never have done this! We know the Father could have stopped this, but He did not. We don't need to question why, that is for sure! Since He did not stop it, there must be a reason why. It will be breathtaking to see how all of this unfolds.

"People are still mocking Him! Are they truly bonkers? He is nailed to a cross. They think He can't fight back. They sure are some cruel people down there. No regard at all for the Man who created them. What thankless people they are.

"He is speaking again. He just said, *'Eli, Eli, lama sabachthani?'* which means, *'My God, my God, why hast thou forsaken me?'*

"Impossible! We were talking about this before and were trying to figure out what this meant. He knows, we know, and all of Heaven knows that God would not forsake Him. Not in His character. He doesn't do things like that. Love is what exudes out of His Being, and not forsaking others is just part of that. Of course, it is others who forsake Him; and He honors their choice."

"Hey, fellas," Elap interjected. "Remember when we watched those Jewish parents as they taught their kids? One thing they always did was have their children memorize Scripture. They knew the importance of getting God's Word into them at a very young age and letting it infuse their whole being with truth that would last them all the days of their lives. Something just hit me. I was listening to some of those children recite the Scriptures to their parents. Guess what? *'My God, my God, why hast thou forsaken me'* is a direct quote from one of the Psalms!

"There were times when I would watch those youngsters struggle to repeat verses to their parents. Their folks had them memorize whole chapters to capture the beautiful and graceful flow that God has put in His Word. Sometimes, that child would stand there with that stricken look on their face. They couldn't remember it. So their gracious, loving parent would give them the first word, or first couple of words, and then what would happen? You guessed it. The whole verse and chapter would come flowing off of their lips! That child was so happy and so were their parents!

"As you might have figured out *'My God, my God, why hast thou forsaken me'* is the very first verse of Chapter 22 in the book of Psalms! So, you know what that means? We had better find out what the rest of that chapter says:

PSALM 22

My God, my God, why hast thou forsaken me? why art thou so far from helping me, and from the words of my roaring?

O my God, I cry in the day time, but thou hearest not; and in the night season, and am not silent.

But thou art holy, O thou that inhabitest the praises of Israel.

Our fathers trusted in thee: they trusted, and thou didst deliver them.

They cried unto thee, and were delivered: they trusted in thee, and were not confounded.

But I am a worm, and no man; a reproach of men, and despised of the people.

All they that see me laugh me to scorn: they shoot out the lip, they shake the head, saying,

He trusted on the LORD that he would deliver him: let him deliver him, seeing he delighted in him.

But thou art he that took me out of the womb: thou didst make me hope when I was upon my mother's breasts.

I was cast upon thee from the womb: thou art my God from my mother's belly.

Be not far from me; for trouble is near; for there is none to help.

Many bulls have compassed me: strong bulls of Bashan have beset me round.

They gaped upon me with their mouths, as a ravening and a roaring lion.

I am poured out like water, and all my bones are out of joint: my heart is like wax; it is melted in the midst of my bowels.

My strength is dried up like a potsherd; and my tongue cleaveth to my jaws; and thou hast brought me into the dust of death.

For dogs have compassed me: the assembly of the wicked have inclosed me: they pierced my hands and my feet.

I may tell all my bones: they look and stare upon me.

They part my garments among them, and cast lots upon my vesture.

But be not thou far from me, O LORD: O my strength, haste thee to help me.

Deliver my soul from the sword; my darling from the power of the dog.

Save me from the lion's mouth: for thou hast heard me from the horns of the unicorns.

I will declare thy name unto my brethren: in the midst of the congregation will I praise thee.

Ye that fear the LORD, praise him; all ye the seed of Jacob, glorify him; and fear him, all ye the seed of Israel.

For he hath not despised nor abhorred the affliction of the afflicted; neither hath he hid his face from him; but when he cried unto him, he heard.

My praise shall be of thee in the great congregation: I will pay my vows before them that fear him.

> The meek shall eat and be satisfied: they shall praise the LORD that seek him: your heart shall live for ever.
>
> All the ends of the world shall remember and turn unto the LORD: and all the kindreds of the nations shall worship before thee.
>
> For the kingdom is the LORD's: and he is the governor among the nations.
>
> All they that be fat upon earth shall eat and worship: all they that go down to the dust shall bow before him: and none can keep alive his own soul.
>
> A seed shall serve him; it shall be accounted to the LORD for a generation.
>
> They shall come, and shall declare his righteousness unto a people that shall be born, that he hath done this.

"Did you see what I just saw? The wicked have surrounded Jesus and have pierced Him in His hands and feet! The Truth was in broad daylight! This was foretold by God a few thousand years ago! God knew this was going to happen. That is why He didn't send legions of angels to get Jesus out of there. We need to figure out why all of this has occurred.

"Here is something else to think about. There are Jews everywhere down there around the cross. Look at their faces. They are doing some serious contemplating. I bet I can tell you what is going on. Since Jesus said, *'My God, my God why hast thou forsaken me,'* it looks like their hooves are moving fast in their heads! We can see them thinking. We can see them engrossed in something. I am pretty sure they are reciting Psalm 22 in their heads! Once that first verse was said by Jesus, we know many of them went from verse 2 to verse 3 and all the way through to the end in their minds.

"Hey, look at their faces. Their eyes are getting big! It looks like the mane is standing up on the back of their necks! They are staring at Jesus. They must have just reached that part of the chapter where it says they will pierce Him in His hands and His feet! Look at them! They are realizing it is coming true right before their eyes!! They are literally standing on the precipice of history! Messiah is before them. The verses they have read all of their lives have just come to fruition. The prophecies of the Most High God have now been fulfilled, and there is no way on God's green earth they can miss it. This will lead many of them to believe in Yeshua as their Messiah. It's written all over their faces. Praise ye the Lord!

"Jesus is speaking once more saying, *'It is finished.'* His work is done. He completed what He came to do for His Father. Obedient to the end. Listen! He is speaking some last words, *'Father into thy hands I commend my Spirit.'*

"What a Savior! Nothing like Him in the entire universe. Putting His Spirit right back into the hands of God. What a simple, yet powerful example He leaves to all. If everyone down there would just put their lives in the hands of Almighty God and let Him mold and shape them the way that He wants to use them to bring the most glory to Himself, what amazing lives they would live. Any other choice besides that will never, ever lead to a fulfilled life.

"Jesus just took His last breath. Amazing to watch. But God is now rocking the world. The veil at the Temple has just now split in two. Some graves of the great, faithful saints of old have opened, and they are now walking around Jerusalem! Look at that! This is truly extraordinary; but truly, those people have no clue what they have just done to the Son of God.

"It seems almost surreal. It is like He was born to die. He was falsely accused, and it led to His death. Now, we know this was foretold in the book of Psalms, so we also know there is a rhyme and reason to all of this."

"Something isn't right here. They are burying Him in a tomb. Jesus can't die. We know that. Of course, they don't realize that. But why are they burying Him in a tomb?" Onyx questioned.

"I guess we better keep our eyes open and see where this is heading!

"Looks like the Father is sending an angel to do some more of His bidding. That angel is heading straight towards the tomb of Jesus. Now the earth is rocking again! God does not mess around!

"But the tomb is empty!! We should have known. You can't keep the greatest Man ever down! That is for sure! Death can't hold Him! He is God!!

"Those people need to realize something: Once Jesus conquered death, all of them are going to conquer death, too. They will either conquer it to Heaven or they will conquer it to Hell, but they will be conquering it. That is exciting but sobering, as well. Are they paying attention?

"As we know, Jesus is always showing us something. He is a teacher at heart. He loves so much that He wants to show others that love. Do you notice how He keeps appearing to people after the Resurrection?"

"Yes, He appeared to Mary at the tomb, He appeared to other women who had already left the tomb, and He appeared to a couple of His disciples on the road to Emmaus," Ivory noted.

"Why won't the other disciples believe them when they say He has risen from the dead?" Onyx inquired.

"That sure is a stubborn lot down there! No worries, though. We know Jesus will convince them somehow!

"There He goes. He just appeared to His disciples! They now know, and there should be no turning back for them. They have seen the resurrected Christ, and they should be faithful to Him until their very last breath.

"He just appeared to over 500 of the brethren at once! That is so like Him. Those folks will have no excuse now. He didn't do this behind closed doors. He did it out in the wide open, so no one down there could doubt or dismiss what He has done. He died publicly, He rose from the dead publicly, and these people need to live their lives publicly for Him, as well!

"Jesus is giving His disciples some last instructions now, *'But ye shall receive power, after that the Holy Ghost is come upon you: and ye shall be witnesses unto me both in Jerusalem, and in all Judaea, and in Samaria, and unto the uttermost part of the earth.'*

"Is He amazing or *what*?"

"There is no *what* about it! Yes, He most certainly is! He cares about them so, so much. He promises to send the Comforter to tend to them. He would never leave them alone. They may feel alone at times, I gather, but they will never, ever be alone. His character is stunning. His graciousness is so real. I do hope they never forget that, but their track record isn't good. Those folks on earth have the propensity to walk away from Him at a moment's notice. But this time, He went to visit the whole nation; and many of the Jews saw Him. This time they touched Him. This time they saw Him perform miracles. This time they saw Him after He arose from the dead. This time it should be different, and they shouldn't walk away from Him ever again," Ivory contended.

"Look, fellas! He just ascended from earth! He is leaving them and coming home! It seems like His work is finished down there. He has done His job. He died for the sins of the whole world. Every sin ever committed by anyone at any time has now been paid for. Stunning. What will those people do with that? They need nothing else to be right with God. Nothing. What a remarkable life He lived down there. Brilliant. Spectacular. Praise be to God!!"

"This will not be the last time people see Jesus," Ivory said.

 "Wow! Remember that sense of triumph over sin and death? That promise of life to the world?" Onyx exclaimed.

"Absolutely! We thought all would turn out okay for mankind, but they still needed a spur in that right direction," Ivory retorted.

"Ouch! Hurts just thinking about that," Onyx winced.

"Yes, because God was not about to let sin have the last grip on man. He wanted truth to grip them instead," Ivory clarified as they moved along.

Chapter 9
Last but Not Least

"*Very interesting. Now the Comforter* has gone to be with the people of earth. Looks like the Father has sent Him to convict the world of sin, righteousness, and the Judgment to come. The Father really doesn't want those people who are made in His image to walk away from Him again. He will use the Holy Ghost to bring them conviction of sin, so hopefully they will turn to Jesus for forgiveness. He wants to show them the truth, so they will come running to the Lord. This is a grand plan! It should work, but those folks down there are a squirrely lot. God so wants people to live righteously; but if they really understood that Judgment was coming, they sure would be living differently," Crimson concluded.

"So He is going to send them the Counselor Who will encourage and exhort them to live holy lives. He is going to walk right alongside them. They will never be alone. Never. There will not come a time when any believer in Jesus will walk by himself. Now they won't be seeing Him, so they need to know this piece of truth. I sure hope they don't forget this nugget of Truth that will be with them for a lifetime!

"The other interesting thing to watch is when people get saved. The Spirit takes up residence in them! He lives in them! He loves them that much. He wants to be that close to them. They are literally sealed in the Spirit of God. And as we know, there is no breaking a seal that God makes! What power and compassion He has. He has done so very much for those people. I wish they could see it from our perch up here. He loves them so very much. It is literally an unconditional and everlasting love that will go on forever and ever and ever.

"He is going to guide those people into truth. Truth just emanates out of Him. The lies on earth will continue for a while. Satan does his dirty work. God wants everyone to have truth. We can easily see that. The battle continues between truth and lies. We know God will be the ultimate winner, but who will be winning in the short term? Do those people even know there is a battle going on? This seems a little frustrating to me, but that is why I am not God.

"We should know by now that Satan will try and mess up what Jesus has done. Satan can't change it, but I'm sure he is going to try and deceive people so they will not get the whole truth about what Jesus did for them. He will give them half-truths or just a smidgen of truth wrapped in a lie, and they will buy it. Distorting the truth is what he loves to do. And he will even convince people they are bringing glory to Jesus when, in reality, he has deceived them into worshiping a different Jesus! What an interesting clash this will be. Now we know who wins in the end, but literally, souls are at stake here.

"As the Spirit begins to move in these people's lives, we just know they are going to exemplify love, joy, peace, long-suffering, gentleness, goodness, faith, meekness, and temperance. We can see that this battle will take place between the Spirit and the flesh. God wants to mold and shape His followers, and Satan wants to try and mess it all up. They can truthfully be new creations if they allow the Spirit to completely work in and through them. The Spirit is going to empower them to speak boldly until their very last breath. The only question is will they follow His commands?"

 "There is no better gift than having the Comforter as the guarantee of an unbreakable covenant with God! But that is a choice they get to make," Crimson remarked.

68

"And those who didn't make that choice before Jerusalem was destroyed faced some very serious consequences. Puts a burr in my saddle every time I think back on all of that," Onyx shuddered.

"We need to be taking some last steps, too. Let's keep going," Crimson urged.

Chapter 10
The Last Stand

"**Looks like the Romans are** ransacking Jerusalem," Onyx observed. "The Roman General Titus does not know what he is doing. He is messing with God, and you don't mess with God and get away with it. It just doesn't work that way. They will probably build a monument for Titus one day to commemorate this event. He has no clue he is coming over to this side.

"Titus wants to get inside of the temple to capture the Jews who are hiding there. Jesus told His disciples that there would not *'be left one stone upon another, that shall not be thrown down.'* Its stones are massive and weigh up to 400 tons! Keep your eyes on that temple, fellas. I think we're about to see prophecy come true.

"Titus just gave the orders for battering rams to take down the Temple's western wall. The Jews inside are protecting the Lord's house with their lives! Titus is having no success. The wall is holding firm.

"Now they are erecting ladders to get in by climbing over the wall! We doubt that will work, but he is trying anyway. The Jews are pushing their ladders backwards, and Roman soldiers are hitting the ground. Titus is not happy that his soldiers are falling to their death.

"Titus has a different idea. He is giving orders to set the Temple gates ablaze. That appears to be working. His soldiers are flooding into the Temple mount. Mission accomplished. Now Titus is giving orders to put out the fire. But wait! Why are the stones still left standing?"

"I think we're about to find out!" Elap declared. "The history God wrote in advance is about to come true. Look! That Roman soldier is furious with the Jews. He is defying orders. He refuses to put the fire out and is carrying a torch. He is throwing it into that window!"

"Now the entire Temple is burning," Onyx lamented. "All the gold and silver inside are melting into the cracks between the stones of the Temple. The stones will need to be dismantled one by one to recover the silver and gold. Not one stone will be left standing upon another. They will all be taken down. The prophecy will come true to its smallest detail. The Temple has served its purpose. God has a new temple in mind.

"Not only has Titus destroyed the Temple, but he has taken spoils from it. I bet he will show them off one day. When you steal God's Menorah, it's like poking your finger into the eyes of God. That is not a smart move by Titus. I sure hope he realizes that he can repent of what he has done.

"The destruction of the Temple doesn't have to be Titus' last act. He has a very big eternal choice to make."

"The people should have taken Jesus' warnings seriously, but they were slow to listen," Elap said.

"Too true," Onyx agreed. "So the next thing God did was give them His last words as a lasting reminder to keep them headed in the right direction in life."

"And we need to be moving straight ahead, too," Elap prodded.

Chapter 11
The Last and Final Word

"*Time continues to progress,*" *Ivory* began, "and people really only need to figure out something very simple as their lives wind down on the blue planet: Is there a God, and has He spoken to us? People need to find that out! Once they have, then everything else, pretty much, falls into place.

"We know that God is not going to leave those people completely alone. He has given them eyes and brains. They need to read and understand. If they do that, it will give them a great head start in living for the Lord and finishing well for Him.

"We can tell they have already accepted all of the Old Testament by the time of Jesus' birth, but we also know the Holy Spirit has been working through some other people to do some more writing. He is going to use the letters written by the known apostles and their associates of the day. Their writings are in wide circulation and their teachings are consistent with the teachings of the Old Testament prophets.

"We know that God is always the organizer. If He can write a book, then He can put a book together! Matter of fact, He can keep that book together throughout all of history to make sure people in all ages have the words of the Most High God in their hands. They will need eternal truth to deal with the earthly and eternal lies they are being told. They will need God's words. They will need His Book; and now, they have it. So the question remains: What are they going to do with it?

INSPIRATION OF SCRIPTURE

And that from a child thou hast known the holy scriptures, which are able to make thee wise unto salvation through faith which is in Christ Jesus.

All scripture is given by inspiration of God, and is profitable for doctrine, for reproof, for correction, for instruction in righteousness:

That the man of God may be perfect, thoroughly furnished unto all good works.

~

For the prophecy came not in old time by the will of man: but holy men of God spake as they were moved by the Holy Ghost.

"God has literally breathed His book into existence. The Holy Spirit moved through its writers to have them write like He wanted them to. He isn't taking any chances. He needs His Word in people's hands. He needs them to know truth. He can't play around with this. He is the Painter, and He just uses the paint brush of the writer's hands to give all those people the words of the wonderful God of the universe! That is how important His Word is. That is why people need to know His Book. It's like a light shining in the darkness of winter. Truth is always like that. Listen to what Holy Writ says about His Word:

THE WORD OF GOD

Thy word is a lamp unto my feet, and a light unto my path.

I have sworn, and I will perform it, that I will keep thy righteous judgments.

I am afflicted very much: quicken me, O LORD, according unto thy word.

Accept, I beseech thee, the freewill offerings of my mouth,

O LORD, and teach me thy judgments.

My soul is continually in my hand: yet do I not forget thy law.

The wicked have laid a snare for me: yet I erred not from thy precepts.

Thy testimonies have I taken as an heritage for ever: for they are the rejoicing of my heart.

I have inclined mine heart to perform thy statutes alway, even unto the end.

I hate vain thoughts: but thy law do I love.

Thou art my hiding place and my shield: I hope in thy word.

Depart from me, ye evil-doers: for I will keep the commandments of my God.

Uphold me according unto thy word, that I may live: and let me not be ashamed of my hope.

~

This book of the law shall not depart out of thy mouth; but thou shalt meditate therein day and night, that thou mayest observe to do according to all that is written therein: for then thou shalt make thy way prosperous, and then thou shalt have good success.

Have not I commanded thee? Be strong and of a good courage; be not afraid, neither be thou dismayed: for the LORD thy God is with thee whithersoever thou goest.

~

I will delight myself in thy statutes: I will not forget thy word.

Deal bountifully with thy servant, that I may live, and keep thy word.

Open thou mine eyes, that I may behold wondrous things out of thy law.

~

For the word of God is quick, and powerful, and sharper than any twoedged sword, piercing even to the dividing asunder of soul and spirit, and of the joints and marrow, and is a discerner of the thoughts and intents of the heart.

~

But his delight is in the law of the LORD; and in his law doth he meditate day and night.

~

The fear of the LORD is clean, enduring for ever: the judgments of the LORD are true and righteous alto-gether.

More to be desired are they than gold, yea, than much fine gold: sweeter also than honey and the honeycomb.

~

The law of thy mouth is better unto me than thousands of gold and silver.

> And the word of the LORD was precious in those days; there was no open vision.
>
> ~
>
> He that goeth forth and weepeth, bearing precious seed, shall doubtless come again with rejoicing, bringing his sheaves with him.

"And when these folks know the Word of God, obey the Word of God, and live out the Word of God, it leads to wisdom. When they apply biblical knowledge to their lives, then that is wisdom.

"That is what everyone down there needs. Listen to what God has written about it:

THE WISDOM OF GOD

But where shall wisdom be found? and where is the place of understanding?

Man knoweth not the price thereof; neither is it found in the land of the living.

The depth saith, It is not in me: and the sea saith, It is not with me.

It cannot be gotten for gold, neither shall silver be weighed for the price thereof.

It cannot be valued with the gold of Ophir, with the precious onyx, or the sapphire.

The gold and the crystal cannot equal it: and the exchange of it shall not be for jewels of fine gold.

No mention shall be made of coral, or of pearls: for the price of wisdom is above rubies.

The topaz of Ethiopia shall not equal it, neither shall it be valued with pure gold.

Whence then cometh wisdom? and where is the place of understanding?

~

Happy is the man that findeth wisdom, and the man that getteth understanding.

For the merchandise of it is better than the merchandise of silver, and the gain thereof than fine gold.

She is more precious than rubies: and all the things thou canst desire are not to be compared unto her.

~

The proverbs of Solomon the son of David, king of Israel;

To know wisdom and instruction; to perceive the words of understanding;

To receive the instruction of wisdom, justice, and judgment, and equity;

To give subtilty to the simple, to the young man knowledge and discretion.

A wise man will hear, and will increase learning; and a man of understanding shall attain unto wise counsels:

To understand a proverb, and the interpretation; the words of the wise, and their dark sayings.

The fear of the LORD is the beginning of knowledge: but fools despise wisdom and instruction.

~

Trust in the LORD with all thine heart; and lean not unto thine own understanding.

In all thy ways acknowledge him, and he shall direct thy paths.

Be not wise in thine own eyes: fear the LORD, and depart from evil.

~

Wisdom is the principal thing; therefore get wisdom: and with all thy getting get understanding.

~

But unto them which are called, both Jews and Greeks, Christ the power of God, and the wisdom of God.

Because the foolishness of God is wiser than men; and the weakness of God is stronger than men.

For ye see your calling, brethren, how that not many wise men after the flesh, not many mighty, not many noble, are called:

But God hath chosen the foolish things of the world to confound the wise; and God hath chosen the weak things of the world to confound the things which are mighty.

~

If any of you lack wisdom, let him ask of God, that giveth to all men liberally, and upbraideth not; and it shall be given him.

~

But the wisdom that is from above is first pure, then peaceable, gentle, and easy to be intreated, full of mercy and good fruits, without partiality, and without hypocrisy.

"If God is ever going to use those people like He wants to, they need wisdom. They need to study the Word of God and apply it to their lives, or they won't stand a chance against the enemy of God. They need all the godly wisdom they can get for the last days ahead."

"God's Word told them everything they needed to know. Profound, if you ask me," Crimson remarked.

"'Oh, the depth of the riches both of the wisdom and knowledge of God!'" Ivory exclaimed.

"And they needed that wisdom for what happened next. We had hoped it would be the last attack of its kind; but sadly, the enemy kept up his same old tactics and schemes against God's people," Crimson lamented.

Chapter 12
Last Week's News

"*Of there is one common* denominator we can see down there, it is the persecution of the Jewish people almost everywhere they go. That is crazy. Why do you think people want to do that to them?" Crimson wondered.

"Well, let's see what history shows us. Pharaoh tried to wipe out the children born to Jewish women. That is just evil—and that is what he was—but it didn't stop the plans of God. He raised up the faithful servant Moses to deliver them during those days. The Jews also faced the threat of annihilation during the Persian Empire, but God thwarted those plans, too. And there was the slaying of all the young children in Bethlehem when Jesus was born. But the attacks on the Jews didn't stop there.

"Many times throughout history, the Jews have been expelled from Jerusalem. The Temple has been destroyed twice. The Spanish Inquisition was a terrible time for many Jews. Certain European cities had ghettoes that were just for the Jews. People disliked them so much, they tried to put them in their own little corner and keep them away from the rest of society. There really is an anti-Semitic hatred for them. Why is it like this?

"The *pogroms* against the Jews were wicked times. They were 'violent riots against the Jews.' Sometimes they seemed to be spontaneous; and other times, they seemed premeditated. People would try to destroy Jewish neighborhoods and businesses. They were very successful in their own eyes because these attacks caused many Jews to flee and emigrate to different countries. There is just such evil and wickedness behind all of that; and, of course, we know who authored those attacks.

"One of the underlying forces going on here is that people consider the Jews to be beneath their level. They aren't as high up the food chain, so to speak, as they are. As long as people believe the lies of evolution and its *survival of the fittest*, anything is possible. They can literally justify any conclusion they want to against any people group if they do not understand God's perspective towards the people He has created. His Word always has the answers that people should truly be looking for.

MADE IN THE IMAGE OF GOD

For thou hast possessed my reins: thou hast covered me in my mother's womb.

I will praise thee; for I am fearfully and wonderfully made: marvellous are thy works; and that my soul knoweth right well.

My substance was not hid from thee, when I was made in secret, and curiously wrought in the lowest parts of the earth.

Thine eyes did see my substance, yet being unperfect; and in thy book all my members were written, which in continuance were fashioned, when as yet there was none of them.

How precious also are thy thoughts unto me, O God! how great is the sum of them!

If I should count them, they are more in number than the sand: when I awake, I am still with thee.

~

Before I formed thee in the belly I knew thee;

~

[F]or the LORD seeth not as man seeth; for man looketh on the outward appearance, but the LORD looketh on the heart.

~

So God created man in his own image, in the image of God created he him; male and female created he them.

~

The spirit of God hath made me, and the breath of the Almighty hath given me life.

~

How much less to him that accepteth not the persons of princes, nor regardeth the rich more than the poor? for they all are the work of his hands.

~

Know ye that the LORD he is God: it is he that hath made

> us, and not we ourselves; we are his people, and the sheep of his pasture.
>
> Even every one that is called by my name: for I have created him for my glory, I have formed him; yea, I have made him.

"All lives matter to the Holy One. He created every one of them. Could He make it any clearer for the people roaming earth? They seem to like coming up with separate categories down there. They especially like those different racial categories. I don't get it. That is a non-issue with the Father. Everyone is made in His image. Period. End of sentence. No need to go any further. No need to subdivide that. Tall, short, fat, skinny, straight-A student, failing out of school, great athlete, bench warmer, rich dude, pauper, and every shade of skin color are *ALL* made in the image of God. Satan sure has done a masterful job of tricking people, so they don't realize the wonderful thing God has done in creating all of mankind!

"Can anyone imagine Jewish practices not being allowed in Jerusalem, of all places?! That actually happened during the time of Antiochus IV Epiphanes. He took over the holy sites in Jerusalem and forbade many of the Jewish religious practices. He pillaged the Temple and burned all the scrolls of the Torah he could find. That is as diabolical as it gets. He even banned Jewish Sabbaths and feast days. You would think that when he set up the statue of Zeus on the altar in the Temple and sacrificed pigs to Zeus, he knew he couldn't poke his finger in God's eye any more than that. What blasphemy! Did he really think he would get away with that?

"At different points in history, we saw the Jews being murdered or expelled from various countries. England, France, and Austria should have treated them so much better than they did. The Polish people were so generous by taking them in.

"Portugal was especially bad. In the 1500s, its treatment of the Jewish people—and especially those who converted to Christianity—was a very sad time in Portugal's history. Confiscating their goods, slave labor, stretching them on racks, and burning them at the stake were how they dealt with the Jews. They finally drove them out of Portugal in 1536.

"The Jews have always had trouble in Muslim lands. They have had to pay the *jizya* tax; and in some instances wear special articles on their clothing, like a yellow badge on their headgear, to remind people they were Jews. Some Jewish women even had special bells on their shoes so others would know when a Jewish woman was near them. Their hatred for God's chosen people was truly astounding.

"The persecution of the Jews in the Middle East has seemingly been a problem throughout all of history. Palestine has never been a tolerable place for Jewish people. Killing them, forcing them out of their countries, and looting their property seemed so commonplace.

"Since their persecution has gone on for so long, we know the archenemy has to be behind it. It's his *modus operandi*. He always comes to steal, kill, and destroy. These are the fingerprints he leaves everywhere. People just need to dust for them like a good detective does. Satan always leaves his mark behind. He always lets you know that he's been there. He always lets you know he was the main culprit rather than someone just lurking in the shadows. Mayhem is his game, and he plays his game well."

"And then Kristallnacht happened," Elap interjected. "Jewish businesses, buildings, and synagogues had their windows busted out on these nights in Germany and Austria. Glass shards were lying everywhere on the streets. We aren't talking something small here. Over 1,000 synagogues and over 7,000 businesses were damaged or destroyed! The paramilitary forces of the Nazis and many non-Jewish citizens participated in this heinous and hideous activity. Many others just stood by and did nothing. They seemingly could have cared less. But that wasn't all. Jews were massacred, as well. Oh well, another life lost. What's the big deal? These people had no clue that if they let things like this happen, it would only lead to bigger problems and worse treatment of citizens in the days to follow. If a government treats one group of people that way, it can treat all of them that way.

"But the *coup de grâce* the devil had in his back pocket was the Nazi holocaust. Satan must have thought it would work, but no one can thwart the plans of God. We always know the devil tries to defeat God's purposes, but we also know he will never succeed."

"The Nazis tried to wipe out the Jews with their death squads. These paramilitary death squads were mostly used in the lands that the Nazis conquered. They didn't care if they took civilian Jews captive or not. They wanted dead Jews, and they got them," Crimson proclaimed.

"These squads literally went door to door in buildings to take the men away. Once the men were gone, fear would overtake the women and children. They could hear the cars drive up and stop. They could hear the clicking of their boots coming down the hallway. They would hear the knocking on doors and just hope it wasn't their door they were knocking on. They could hear the families being dragged off, and they would stay behind their own doors and do nothing. Fear had gripped them. Satan had done his job, but we know he will never ultimately succeed.

"But the devious pawn of Satan, Mr. Hitler, was not done. It was time for the Final Solution. Here was a man, made in the image of God, who literally wanted to wipe out other people made in the image of God. This makes no sense to me. I totally understand that when a life is turned over to Satan, anything is possible, but how could he get any joy from destroying people whom God had made? I don't understand this kind of wickedness, and I don't want to.

"No one wakes up one day and just comes to the conclusion that they want to wipe out an entire people group. This is incremental. This happens over time. They allow the seeds of hatred to take over little by little. The thoughts of these folks must be evil. They are not setting their mind on the things of God. God thinks about them, and they think about evil. This is crazy. They let sin consume them and turn them into completely different persons.

"We can look down and see that the Nazis have become even more wicked. They used to go to the Jews to kill them, but now they are bringing the Jews to them! So bring the victims to yourselves under false pretenses, but know that you are literally leading lambs to the slaughter. Where are their consciences? Don't they care? What if the shoe was on the other foot, or the *yarmulke* was on their head? Would they want to be treated this way? I just don't understand those people. This is all so very infuriating to see.

"I can see they are calling this the *Shoah* or the Holocaust. *Shoah* means 'the catastrophe' and *holocaust* means 'whole' and 'burnt.' What an absolutely evil way to speak about any human being that God has created. This is wickedness like I have never seen before. Since God wiped out the world during the days of Noah for all of the wicked imaginations of their hearts and the actions they did, then why isn't He doing something now?

"I know. That is a bad statement. He is always doing something. His love is amazing. I know He hears the prayers of the Jews. I know He even hears the prayers of the Jews for Mr. Hitler himself. Some of those Jews have a compassion that resonates out of them, which is literally out of this world.

"If it were me, I would be wiping those Nazis out with a flood, a hurricane, a few lightning strikes, an earthquake, and for good measure a nice tsunami from the North Sea right on top of them to finish them off!! But that's why, for one of many reasons, I'm not God and don't want to be. He knows what He's doing. If we have learned anything, it's that we can trust His judgments. He hasn't been wrong yet; and He never, ever, ever will be. I hope those inhabitants on planet Earth will figure it all out before it's too late.

"Hitler and his comrades are so evil that it isn't just the Jews they are killing. Gypsies, the mentally and physically handicapped, POWs, and seemingly anyone else who does not fit Hitler's idea that the Aryan race is the Master race is in for trouble at the hands of the Nazis. The Nordic or whiter-skinned people are considered the highest of all races. They are the best of the best. They have evolved further along the evolutionary track than darker-skinned people, so they are the cream of the crop. They are the crème de la crème. They are the elite. They are the noble class, and no one is even close to them. So it is best that we get rid of these *inferior folks* so they don't make the mistake of interbreeding with our elite, blue-blooded class.

"What a bunch of horse manure with some hogwash on the side. That is total drivel. Looks to me like Hitler has never read his Bible. Or maybe he has, and he didn't like what it said. By not following the commands of the Lord, he has followed the commands of Satan. As we know, anything is possible when that happens.

"Just to prove that point—and I am not always the best at counting—it looks like two-thirds of the Jews have been killed in Europe now. Adding in the other people that the Third Reich also killed during this genocide, it looks like upward of 11 million people have been murdered by them. That is nuts. No concern at all for the value of a human life that God has created.

"I guess what really disturbs me is that out of those 11 million people, there are right around 1 million Jewish children who have been murdered, too. They have slaughtered that many kids. Exterminated them. Got rid of them. Destroyed them. Those butchers. They have no regard for the Lord. Kids just want to laugh, play, make friends, play some sports, and enjoy God's wonderful creation. Then their parents get the opportunity to teach them all about the God who created them. All of them done away with. No chance to grow up and live like these hooligans had the chance to do. They got the chance to have a childhood that led into adulthood. All of those lives snuffed out and extinguished at the hands of these evil men! What is going on down there? How can they literally be so clueless and wicked?"

"Those extermination camps are beyond the pale," Elap explained. "They just do not care about human life. This isn't a concentration camp where they make them work at hard labor.

This is a killing camp. This is where they are going to extinguish someone's life. They have answered the Jewish question in their minds, and they have come up with the wrong answer. It wasn't that the Jews couldn't own businesses or have the same legal status as others; they needed to die. They needed to be wiped off the face of the earth, and the Nazis were bound and determined to do just that. So let the genocide begin.

"What they have done in these camps is, pretty much, downright wicked. It is vicious and abominable. I would call it devilish because the devil is the fallen master behind murder. It's one of his calling cards. But these people are making choices. They are choosing to murder other people. They could walk away. They could lay down their weapons and just walk away. Yes, it would probably mean their heads would be chopped off. Yes, there can be a heavy penalty for doing what is right, but that is what is commanded. Doing right in every situation is what those people down there should be doing."

"Here come the trains," Crimson noticed. "You can just hear the lies they are peddling. Telling those folks that they are going to forced-labor camps when that is not true. They are taking them to the extermination camps. The father of lies is busy again. He is working hard. They don't even care about a human being enough to tell them the truth, so it's no surprise they find it so easy to kill them, as well. No regard for the life God has provided. The trains keep showing up, and the killings continue.

"Shoot them or gas them to death, and then cremate them. Quick and easy. The faster the better. Don't they realize that every time they do that, a soul leaves the body? Don't they realize they are eternal beings? I'm not sure how many people down there realize that at all.

"What is interesting, though, is that God gave all of those people a conscience. It is interesting to watch how many of those soldiers who pulled the trigger and put a well-placed bullet into the skull of a Jew would either commit suicide or go mad later in their lives. They knew it was wrong. They knew that was not what they were created to do with their lives, but they didn't have the backbone. They didn't have the determination. They didn't have the belief in God to stand against the evil that was all around them. In the end, it cost them something, too.

"This is the devil's continual attempt to completely eradicate the Jews. He tried with Haman, Herod, and now with Hitler. He will never succeed. We know that, but I sure hope those folks figure it out.

"And now there is Islam that doesn't want the Jews to exist either. So many of their maps don't even have the nation of Israel on them! The Palestinian Charter still calls for the destruction of Israel. If we have seen one common thread throughout all of history, it is that people hate the Jewish people. Seems like there are people in every generation who want no Jews on planet Earth. I guess they think that will make them happy, but we know that thinking is many furlongs away from reality.

"Remember when the Lord wrote: *'Behold, I have graven thee upon the palms of my hands'*? I mean, how much more valuable can you be to the Lord than having your name engraved upon His palms? He will never forget the Jews. They are the apple of His eye. He has a special purpose and place for them. If only they would realize that and just stop running from Him. They should just stop, turn around, and start running to Him. Then they would see more remarkable things than the parting of the Red Sea! He has given them a choice. We will see what choices they make, as well.

"I know they are being persecuted because of their religious beliefs, and probably for their culture, but we just get the feeling that there is another reason why all of this is happening. We know that the Jews were committed to bringing forth the oracles of God. They had the responsibility to write down and preserve the words of God. So we know Satan would try and wipe the Jews out. We also know that Jesus was Jewish. He would come through the lineage of the Jews. So we know that Satan would literally do anything in his power to stop His birth from occurring. Of course, he failed miserably! He may win some short-term battles, but he will always lose the war with the Most High God.

"The Scriptures declare that the whole earth will be gathered against Jerusalem and Israel in the latter days. That will not be a good time for the people of earth. They should know better. History will have taught them a lesson they didn't learn.

"Do you remember when Jesus said, *'If thou hadst known, even thou, at least in this thy day, the things which belong unto thy peace! but now they are hid from thine eyes. For the days shall come upon thee, that thine enemies shall cast a trench about thee, and compass thee round, and keep thee in on every side, And shall lay thee even with the ground, and thy children within thee; and they shall not leave in thee one stone upon another; because thou knewest not the time of thy visitation'*?

"They missed the first visit from Jesus. The Jews, overall, did not recognize Him as Messiah. He has now given them a homeland again. All the Jews need to do is acknowledge their offenses to their mighty God. They need to seek His face. They just need to believe and say, *'Blessed is He that cometh in the name of the Lord'!* So simple it seems. So easy to see it from this bird's-eye view. I just don't understand why they don't get it. I know they don't like the persecution and derision that seem to come at them from every side. To repent and believe on their Messiah is so simple; yet, so seemingly hard for them to do.

"This will probably not be the last time the Jews are persecuted down there."

 "God always dearly loved the Jews, even when they didn't love Him back. He was always faithful to them!"
"Good point, Crimson," Elap agreed. "His promises last forever."

"Hard things to think back on. Sadly, it wasn't the last time the devil instigated that kind of trouble for them down there," Crimson replied as they continued toward their destination.

Chapter 13
The Last Signs

*"**T**ime sure moves fast down* on that planet. You would think that from the time of Christ, those inhabitants of the third rock from the sun would spend their time getting to know Him. Learn all they can about Him. Talk to their elders. Research. Study. But it looks like they have other ideas. They are focused on the things of the earth. And they sure like to invent things! They must get some kind of rush from figuring out what God already knows!" Onyx observed.

"During the first millennium—from Jesus' birth to 1,000 A.D.—they have invented or discovered how to use woodblock printing, paper, algebra, steel, hops, coffee, horseshoes, stirrups, magnetic compasses, chess, and gunpowder!

"Now these don't seem like much to us since we already know that God is all-knowing and literally knows everything, but discovering them must have been kind of neat. I'm wondering if those inventions will point people towards the Creator of all, or will they just feed their egos for having discovered something? It seems like that is how it works in their world. People do so much for themselves and so little for the Lord.

"I'm not sure gunpowder is a great invention. Those people really do like war down there. The Jews are being dispersed from their homeland, and Christianity is on the rise. It is moving into many different pockets of the world. People are seeing their need for Jesus.

"But Islam has made a move, as well. It has stepped out and made major inroads into the nations of the world. Muslims are conquering territories and spreading their religion. They now have a presence in the Middle East, the Arabian Peninsula, to the China border, as well as into Northern Africa. We get the feeling that they are going to be players on the world stage all the way until the *Last Ride.*

"During the second millennium—from 1,000 A.D. until now—the printing press, telegraph, photography, telephone, television, computer, satellite, Internet, calculus, genetics, atomic theory, DNA, plastic, assembly line, sliced bread, bicycle, steam engine, internal combustion engine, cars, steam locomotive, human flight and commercial air travel, space shuttle, firearms, tanks, submarines, rockets, and nuclear weapons have all been invented! What a millennium!!

"Those folks sure have discovered a lot about how God designed things to work. Science is really just figuring out how God made things. Most scientists understand that. For the others, it is just *ego city* as they try and patent what God has supplied the parts and knowledge for! They're in for a big shock when they meet the real Creator and Designer face to face!

"I am wondering if the inhabitants of earth are really getting closer to God. Seems like there is a lot of wandering going on. A lot of seeking the things of the world to bring them pleasure. We can tell from up here that is a wasted pursuit. It will only bring them heartache, just as it has in previous millennia. I sure wish they could see it from our vantage point. They would sure think and act a lot differently."

"Genghis Khan, Marco Polo, Thomas Aquinas, Leonardo da Vinci, Ferdinand Magellan, Joan of Arc, William Shakespeare, Christopher Columbus, Galileo, Michelangelo, Martin Luther, Henry VIII, Pocahontas, Isaac Newton, Rembrandt, Benjamin Franklin, Thomas Jefferson, George Washington, Paul Revere, Napoleon, Mozart, Bach, Thomas Edison, Abraham Lincoln, Charles Darwin, Nikola Tesla, Van Gogh, Beethoven, and Karl Marx all lived during the second millennium. They have all passed over to this side now. Their days of meandering on planet Earth are long gone. So many of them wished they could have lived their lives over, but alas, it was not to be. One life. One earthly death. One long eternity. Were they ready?" Ivory questioned.

"The 20th century arrived on the scene in some momentous ways; but now in the 21st century, the population of the world has exploded to over seven billion people! And God wants to see all of those souls get saved. I sure hope those Christians down there see their responsibility and the opportunities they have to spread the Word. We know some of them will get it, but others will be more infatuated with the creation rather than the Creator," Onyx declared.

"Looking down from on high, there is nothing like the last century. It is almost like everything has hit acceleration mode. Like it is turbocharged. The pace has picked up. Almost like earth is barreling towards a final conclusion, but people don't realize it. They don't realize there is a dead end ahead; and once they hit it, they will arrive at the throne of God. Heaven or Hell. Their choice. And that choice needs to be made now.

"A major shift seems to be taking place down there. Two amazingly deadly world wars. We can tell that instead of letting people just live their lives, like most people want to do, control seems to be much more in play than in previous centuries. People want to control others and, in essence, control the world.

"People are also very big on attaching their identity to their nation or homeland. For many, it seems to be more important than their attachment to God. We can see it in their flags and on their money. We can see it in their sports. It is almost like they will stand up for whatever their country does: right or wrong. And we can tell from being perched far above them that this will not end well. If they do not keep the Lord first in all they do, disaster will strike. I am not sure why they have so dismissed the oracles of God—especially when He has decided to write His eternal truths for people—but they are so easily distracted by the things of the world.

"World War I, the Russian Revolution, Mao's Long March, Hitler's rise to power, World War II, the Korean War, the Six Day War, and Vietnam were all conducted during the last century. Counting isn't my thing either, but when looking at the genocide and mass murder of that century, over 150 million people have been slaughtered. Many of those folks just do not care about human life. It is like they are stepping on some dirt or a bug. No big deal. That life is gone, and now we just move on. But we know God has created those people with a conscience. We know that in the deep, dark recesses of their minds and souls, they have to be thinking about what they are doing and what they have done.

"God said, *'Whoso sheddeth man's blood, by man shall his blood be shed: for in the image of God made he man.'* This is very serious business to God. He is not messing around. Those people must not think there is a Judgment Day for their actions, but that day will commence. It will happen. They will be held accountable.

"But one more time, this shows His goodness and graciousness. He gives people time to repent and turn to Him. He loves them dearly, even when they take the life of another human being.

"Remember when He wrote: *'Repent ye therefore, and be converted, that your sins may be blotted out, when the times of refreshing shall come from the presence of the Lord'*? Now that is what He is looking for! That is the humble heart He desires! That is His kind of follower!!

"Franklin Roosevelt, John F. Kennedy, Martin Luther King, Teddy Roosevelt, Ronald Reagan, Mao Zedong, Mahatma Gandhi, Einstein, Lenin, Stalin, Churchill, Hitler, and Picasso all graced the stage during the 20th century. Every life on earth ends the same way: death. *'For the wages of sin is death.'* There is a payment that will be collected for all of the sins that one commits. It will be their lives. They will die. They will take a last breath.

"For the life of me, I cannot figure out why those people won't ask the question: Why do we die? It seems so simple. There is no death up this way. None. It is all eternal life forever and ever and ever. But they die down there. They should be asking why did God create something and allow death to become a part of it. But then, they would have to look in the mirror. They couldn't point a finger at God, like so many of them want to do, and blame Him. They would have to say we have created this. We disobeyed God. We listened to Satan instead of the Most High. We chose to sin, and now there are major consequences for our choices. Graciously and excitingly, God has given them the only option to be right with Him. But that will also be their choice. So many choices down there, and so many consequences for those choices.

"Do you guys remember the answer Jesus gave when He was asked at the Temple about the great signs that would take place in the future, and when that time would be? The people listened intently to His words then, and folks today should do the same.

THE LAST DAYS

Take heed that ye be not deceived: for many shall come in my name, saying, I am Christ; and the time draweth near: go ye not therefore after them.

But when ye shall hear of wars and commotions, be not terrified: for these things must first come to pass; but the end is not by and by.

Then said he unto them, Nation shall rise against nation, and kingdom against kingdom:

And great earthquakes shall be in divers places, and famines, and pestilences; and fearful sights and great signs shall there be from heaven.

But before all these, they shall lay their hands on you, and persecute you, delivering you up to the synagogues, and into prisons, being brought before kings and rulers for my name's sake.

And it shall turn to you for a testimony.

Settle it therefore in your hearts, not to meditate before what ye shall answer:

For I will give you a mouth and wisdom, which all your adversaries shall not be able to gainsay nor resist.

And ye shall be betrayed both by parents, and brethren, and kinsfolks, and friends; and some of you shall they cause to be put to death.

And ye shall be hated of all men for my name's sake.

But there shall not an hair of your head perish.

In your patience possess ye your souls.

And when ye shall see Jerusalem compassed with armies, then know that the desolation thereof is nigh.

Then let them which are in Judaea flee to the mountains; and let them which are in the midst of it depart out; and let not them that are in the countries enter thereinto.

For these be the days of vengeance, that all things which are written may be fulfilled.

But woe unto them that are with child, and to them that give suck, in those days! for there shall be great distress in the land, and wrath upon this people.

And they shall fall by the edge of the sword, and shall be led away captive into all nations: and Jerusalem shall be trodden down of the Gentiles, until the times of the Gentiles be fulfilled.

And there shall be signs in the sun, and in the moon, and in the stars; and upon the earth distress of nations, with perplexity; the sea and the waves roaring;

Men's hearts failing them for fear, and for looking after those things which are coming on the earth: for the powers of heaven shall be shaken.

And then shall they see the Son of man coming in a cloud with power and great glory.

And when these things begin to come to pass, then look up, and lift up your heads; for your redemption draweth nigh.

"I wonder if they are going to open up their eyes and see that what God has written in His Word is coming true right before their very eyes. It is either eyes wide open or eyes wide shut.

"Seismic activity is off the charts down there. That place is rocking. It is shaking like no other time in all of history.

"Andrew, Camille, and Katrina are common terms down there, not because they are family names, but because they are literal destructive events on the blue sphere. These are wake-up calls for the people on earth to come to the Savior, but they tune them out. They hit the snooze button. They want to sleep, and Satan is just fine with that. God wants them wide awake. Who is going to win in getting their attention?

"Influenza, cholera, malaria, AIDS, Ebola, SARS, and weaponized biological plagues are all over the place. These plagues can pass around the world in one plane flight. People are not ready for those diseases, and they are not ready for what happens when they take that last breath after getting one of them.

"The most persecuted people in the world today are the born again followers of the Lord Jesus Christ. They are being murdered by the truckloads every single day, and there is no outcry. There is no fighting back by governments to protect these people; and sadly, in many cases, these regimes are the ones perpetrating the murders against them. More than sixty countries down there are at the forefront in persecuting Christians, and Islamic extremism is leading the way. More Christians have died in the 20th century than in all of the previous centuries combined.

"These persecutors are clueless. They are going to meet the Lord at their death, and no one wants to stand there as a persecutor of His people. But they treated the Jews that way and the Lord that way, so it is no surprise that they treat His followers that way, as well. Oh, but what a way to die: being persecuted!! Now that is the right way to take a last breath. No better way! They truly have no clue what awaits them. It is joy unspeakable for all of eternity! And they will shout for joy for all of eternity!!"

"'Precious in the sight of the LORD is the death of his saints,'" Ivory reflected.

"Yes, and the signs of the last times were beginning to emerge, but too many people were not preparing for eternity," Crimson regretted.

"Remember back then, how you started thinking things through a bit, Crimson? How you began to put the whole picture of salvation together?" Ivory reminded him.

"I think you're putting a bit in my mouth; but, of course, I remember that! It was unforgettable as it all came together. Let's keep moving," Crimson responded.

Chapter 14
The Everlasting Hope

"**H**ey, fellas. **I am beginning** to figure out something here. Now don't call me slow because you know I can gallop with the best of them!" Crimson stated.

"What have you got?" Elap responded.

"I have been wrestling with some things that God's Word says and with some things I have seen on earth. Let me run this past you guys, and let's see if it makes sense."

"Well, it better make biblical sense or we don't have time for it," Elap let Crimson know.

"That, of course, is what I am trying to figure out. Here we go.

"All of those folks down there are sinners. We know it, and they know it. All they have to do is take a look at the Ten Commandments that God wrote for them on those tablets of stone, and they will realize they are in big trouble. God said it, and they disobeyed it.

"But since God is all-knowing, He knew Adam and Eve would fall into sin. And He also knew He would provide a way for them to be right with Him.

"You remember when God gave them judges over the land. Judging is pretty simple. We can watch them run their court-rooms. They know every single person who is alive has sin, but that is not the issue when someone stands before the court. Too many times, people dismiss their sin because they think they are a good person. Judges won't let them off for being good. People are supposed to be good! That is like the basic moral standard for them. They are not supposed to wake up each day and go around breaking laws. If they do, that is where the judge comes in.

"But judges also have boundaries. They can only judge based on the laws that have been passed. So if there is a law on the books, it's the people's job to keep it. If they break the law, they go before the court. The judge looks at the law and looks at the evidence and then, and only then, can that judge find someone guilty.

"So what everyone really needs are their charges dropped. That would be the best. But, of course, judges can't just drop charges. They have to judge by the law. They would be derelict in their duty if they judged in any other way.

"The only other real option is a mediator—someone who could step in between the two parties and take the penalty so the guilty party would not have to pay that penalty."

"I guess while you are figuring out so much, Crimson, you aren't spending much time looking down at planet Earth. Those are some selfish folks down there! Like it's in their DNA or something! They are looking out for number one and if they run over number two, no big deal!" Elap stepped in and continued.

"What someone needs is their record of crime wiped clean, so there is nothing for the judge to judge. Same when it comes to sin. Someone would want their sins wiped clean before they stood before the Judge so, in essence, there wouldn't be any sins for the Judge to judge."

"That is where I am going," Crimson reflected. "Hang with me. So they need their sins removed. Let's go to the Word and see what it says:

WAGES OF SIN

Behold, all souls are mine; as the soul of the father, so also the soul of the son is mine: the soul that sinneth, it shall die.

For the wages of sin is death; but the gift of God is eternal life through Jesus Christ our Lord.

> *For there is one God, and one mediator between God and men, the man Christ Jesus;*
>
> ~
>
> *And I saw the dead, small and great, stand before God; and the books were opened: and another book was opened, which is the book of life: and the dead were judged out of those things which were written in the books, according to their works.*

"God makes things so simple. Sinners die because of their sins. No getting around it. They will die physically, and they will die spiritually because of their transgressions against the Holy God.

"They are going to need forgiveness. Let's take a look at the Old Testament to see if we can get some clues:

ATONEMENT

> *Your lamb shall be without blemish, a male of the first year: ye shall take it out from the sheep, or from the goats:*
>
> ~
>
> *For the life of the flesh is in the blood: and I have given it to you upon the altar to make an atonement for your souls: for it is the blood that maketh an atonement for the soul.*

"So this is what they used to do. The repentant sinner would bring to God a perfect animal without defect or blemish. They would take that animal to the tent of meeting and lay their hands on the animal. They would confess their sins over it. The animal would then be slain at the doorway. The priest would collect the blood, and the blood would be put on the altar. Or if it was the Day of Atonement, the blood would be sprinkled on the mercy seat.

"God would then see that the proper atonement had been made for the sins that were committed. So there were three necessary things to bring before God for the atonement of their sins. It had to be a perfect blood sacrifice. God required a perfect blood sacrifice for the forgiveness of their sins.

"You see, this is what has perplexed me. When we look down and overhear a few of their conversations, we can tell what people are banking on to get to Heaven or to be right with God. It is simple. They think they will be good enough to get to Heaven. They think they will have done enough good works. They think that when God sees all of the good works they have done, He will give them a big bear hug, and they can waltz right through the front door of Heaven for all of eternity. We know that is not the case. He is holy. He is pure. He is without sin. Matter of fact, He hates sin. He despises wickedness. It is literally 100% against His character.

"So we see that Satan has deceived them. Their good works might get them a new job or a raise, or their hard work might earn them more playing time in basketball. Their good works might win them the yard of the month, but none of that is what it takes to be right with the Holy God of the universe.

"But I have finally realized something: All of those sacrificed animals are pointing to something or Someone. They don't sacrifice animals for sins anymore because the Temple was destroyed in 70 AD. Even though God's Word tells the Jews to do that, they don't. That should get someone thinking right there.

"Remember when Luke wrote: *'And the scribes and the Pharisees began to reason, saying, Who is this which speaketh blasphemies? Who can forgive sins, but God alone?'* Only One Person can forgive sins and that is God alone. But He has said He wants a perfect blood sacrifice for those sins that have been committed against Him.

"Now let's remember what the Great Book says:

PERFECT

Who did no sin, neither was guile found in his mouth.

the righteousness of God in him.

For he hath made him to be sin for us, who knew no sin; that we might be made

And ye know that he was manifested to take away our sins; and in him is no sin.

> Seeing then that we have a great high priest, that is passed into the heavens, Jesus the Son of God, let us hold fast our profession.
>
> For we have not an high priest which cannot be touched with the feeling of our infirmities; but was in all points tempted like as we are, yet without sin.

"Now think about this: Jesus has no sin. He is perfect. We know that. So that takes care of the *perfect* part. We know that He humbly laid down His life to go to the cross. The crucifixion is the *sacrifice* part. The final piece of the puzzle is the *blood* part.

"Remember that God's Word says, *'And almost all things are by the law purged with blood; and without shedding of blood is no remission.'* He is reminding them that without the shedding of blood, there can be no remission of sin. But as we have just found out, it must be coupled with perfection and a sacrifice.

"Listen to what else He has to say:

BLOOD

> And from Jesus Christ, who is the faithful witness, and the first begotten of the dead, and the prince of the kings of the earth. Unto him that loved us, and washed us from our sins in his own blood.
>
> But with the precious blood of Christ, as of a lamb without blemish and without spot.
>
> How much more shall the blood of Christ, who through the eternal Spirit offered himself without spot to God, purge your conscience from dead works to serve the living God?
>
> But if we walk in the light, as he is in the light, we have fellowship one with another, and the blood of Jesus Christ his Son cleanseth us from all sin.

"I think we are about to hit one of those eureka moments! This is life changing. This is eternally life changing if those people will wake up and see this. Their earthly lives and their eternal lives will never be the same.

"So only someone sinless could pay for someone else's sins. Only God is sinless, so that would then mean that God has to be willing to pay for the people's sins.

"Of course, that would then mean God must be willing to be the sacrifice for those sins. Without a sacrifice, there is no forgiveness. The Holy Book says even more:

SACRIFICE

And he is the propitiation for our sins: and not for ours only, but also for the sins of the whole world.

Whom God hath set forth to be a propitiation through faith in his blood, to declare his righteousness for the remission of sins that are past, through the forbearance of God.

"Jehovah is a holy God. Period. There is a just side to Him, as well. His justice has to be satiated. It must be satisfied. That is what propitiation is. It is that sacrifice. It is that Substitute paying the penalty for the people's sins. When there is a breach between two parties and peace needs to be reached between them, this is what propitiation does. Two parties come to agreement, and both sides get on the same page. Propitiation means satisfaction. God must be satisfied with the payment for those transgressions in order for those two parties—not to be in the same library and not even to be in the same book—but to be on the same page. Listen again to what He has said, *'Herein is love, not that we loved God, but that he loved us, and sent his Son to be the propitiation for our sins.'*

"Now, hold that thought about love because I am going to come back to it. Let's talk about something a little tougher: blood. People don't like talking about that. People sometimes can't handle seeing it in movies down there. Some guys won't even watch their wife delivering their baby because they cannot handle the blood. Blood can literally make them sick to their stomachs. The human body can manufacture—are you ready for this—17 million red blood cells in one second! Yes, that is true. The human body is an amazing machine that God has made, but did you know that blood brings oxygen and nourishment to their bodies? It also cleanses their bodies of the toxins and impurities that would kill them. Blood brings life and carries away the death for human beings. So blood is actually a cleanser.

"Now watch this: the blood of Christ does the same thing! Faith in His sinless blood sacrifice will bring someone eternal life and cleanse away the sin that would bring their eternal death. His blood brings them life and carries away the death. God has designed blood in the human body for a reason. And He uses that to show what the blood of His Son Jesus will do for anyone who places faith in Him. It is the perfect example to show us how blood brings life, and *His* blood brings eternal life!

"So here is where the hoof meets the road. Let's put this to the test to see if it works:

"**Baptism:** If God says only a sinless blood sacrifice removes sin, can baptism remove sin? Nope! It's a sinful person; water not blood; and there is no death. Baptism can't remove sins.

"**Purgatory:** It's a sinful person in purgatory and not a sinless person; flames not blood; and there is no death. Purgatory cannot expiate sins.

"**Confession:** It's a sinful person supposedly absolving them of sin, so it's not sinless; reciting the *Hail Mary* and *Our Father* prayers rather than depending on the blood; and, of course, there is no death. Going to confession cannot remove sins.

"**Church Membership:** It's not a sinless blood sacrifice, so it cannot remove sins.

"**Atonement in the Garden:** Mormons believe that Jesus atoned for sin in the Garden of Gethsemane. It's the wrong Jesus because they believe he was once a man who became a god. Since all men have sinned, that means it would not have been a sinless sacrifice. There may have been blood in the Garden of Gethsemane, but there was no death; so any so-called atonement in the garden can't remove sins.

"**Five Pillars of Islam or the Weighing Scales:** If someone's good and bad deeds were weighed on the scales in front of Allah, this would not constitute a sinless blood sacrifice.

"**Suffering:** Some people think that suffering is the payment for sins, but it would not be a sinless blood sacrifice, so it cannot remove or expiate sins.

"**Good Deeds:** Nope. Not a sinless blood sacrifice. Their goodness can't remove their sins, but only cover them up.

"**Religious Works:** Mormons do temple work for the dead, but it's not a sinless blood sacrifice. Hinduism offers food to their deities to remove sins. Any religious deed or good work that someone does will never be a sinless blood sacrifice, which means it can't remove their sins.

"God has made it so simple for them. Here is an example: If you took a white t-shirt and tapped it thirty times with a pen or even once with a pen, it is not a clean white T-shirt anymore. Do you remember when He said, *'For whosoever shall keep the whole law, and yet offend in one point, he is guilty of all'*? If they have broken one of His commandments, it is just like they have broken all of them.

"Why don't these people understand? We know how much the Lord loves them. He has put truth all around them, but it is their job to search it out. It is their job to seek. Satan feeds them lies; and sometimes, the lies are much easier to swallow. It is like honey on their lips. It might taste good at first, but too much of it and you will soon be getting sick to your stomach. Same here. These false belief systems all hit the person's pride. They think it is them. They think it is their good works that will make them righteous. They don't understand God's quality of holiness. They don't realize He won't play that game of sin. They need to bring Him the right gift because anything else won't cut it.

"Here's another example. Folks down there worry so much about stealing! If they would just follow God's Laws, it would be so much simpler for them. So they put sensors at the exits of stores to set off the beeper to catch thieves. It would be interesting if God did that! If He put some sensors at the gates of Heaven so that when people walked in, the sensors would only go off if their sins had not been washed away. That would sure be a wake-up call for them. Sadly, it would be too late. They can't make the decision to become born again after they die. It must be made before they die.

"As we can see, so many people on earth have been religiously deceived. They think they have the right answer for when they come face to face with God, but they do not. God has made it so simple. Basic, you might even say. He doesn't want anyone to have a bad meeting with Him. He wants them to have a smooth Judgment Day. I wonder if they realize that.

"Whatever they're depending on cannot remove their sins unless it's the one and only, genuine real-deal, sinless blood sacrifice of Jesus Christ!

"Remember when Isaiah wrote: *'Come now, and let us reason together, saith the LORD: though your sins be as scarlet, they shall be as white as snow; though they be red like crimson, they shall be as wool'?* That is an off the chart *wow*!! Pure and clean and fresh like a nice blizzard! God makes such beautiful snow. Then people make it muddy and drive their cars on it, and it gets all gray. But it is not dirty once He has forgiven those sins. Pure. White. As snow. Perfect. Blood. Sacrifice. Simple!

"The Holy Scriptures state: *'And they overcame him by the blood of the Lamb, and by the word of their testimony; and they loved not their lives unto the death.'* Once they understand what His blood really does, they can't wait to take that last breath and meet the One who shed it for them!!

"The final act is coming. The last call will be given soon. The last words of the last chapter of the last book have been written.

105

Their fulfillment is coming up on the horizon and will be coming true soon enough. If someone doesn't hand Almighty God a perfect blood sacrifice when they meet Him, it will be the last and final worst mistake they will ever make. The end of the road is coming. Jesus went to the ends of the earth to bring them His sacrifice. Their deadline with death is arriving. The choice is theirs. What will they do?"

 "What an unspeakable privilege to be offered ever-lasting life with the King!" Crimson marveled as he thought back.

"He sure wanted to prepare them for a great eternity; but in order for that to happen, they needed to be trained up in the way they should go. They needed to learn how to trust Him and walk in His ways," Elap reminded them as they kept heading toward their destination.

Chapter 15
The Last Generation

"*One of the things we* just love about the Lord is how much He cares for His people. He literally loves them beyond what words will ever be able to describe. So to figure out that love, they must really study His Word," Onyx noted.

"When you love someone, you always set them up to succeed and not to fail. You want the best for them today, tomorrow, and the next day. So when we look at God's Word and watch all of this history on earth, sometimes it is best to go back to the beginning. Back to the first time God did something, which shows us a pattern. Do you realize what the first institution is that God created?

"Interestingly, it is not the church. That wasn't His first institution. For sure, we know it wasn't government. All that institution seems to have done is cause problems throughout the expanse of time, and it probably will until Jesus returns.

"Isn't it fascinating, though, to see so many Christians trying to solve the problems of their countries through government? It is so easy to see the solution from up here. Everywhere we look there is one, and only one, problem. Those countries have a spiritual problem and not a political problem. Human governments like power, and God likes humbleness. For the life of me, I cannot figure out why believers keep running to politicians and political parties to exact change down there. They need to be soul winning and praying if they really want to see change!

"The first institution God made was marriage and the home. That clear and that simple. He knew the proper building block for every society would be the nuclear family of one husband, one wife, and children. As easy as ABC.

"You ever watch those people down there stack playing cards and build things with them?"

"Of course I do, and I've figured out they have way too much time on their hands!" Elap responded.

"That is for sure. So you've seen what happens when they pull a card out from the bottom," Onyx explained. "The whole thing comes tumbling down. That is where they get the term *house of cards*. If something is built on a shaky foundation, it is not going to last for the long haul. It is just like when Jesus talked about them building their house upon rock or their house upon sand. The foundation is the key. If they have a nice mansion built right on top of a Hawaiian beach, they might think it is paradise, but it is going to turn into *Paradise Lost* eventually!"

"That is what God is saying here. Keep that family unit intact. Don't mess it up. A properly structured family will be the bedrock and foundation for a well-run family, which then leads to a well-run society. Do it any other way, and trouble is on the horizon.

"So when we look down there, what do we see? We see people with more than one wife! Even we can tell that is not going to fly! There is no way a husband can give the proper time to each wife, and, of course, the kids would not get enough *dad* time.

"Some societies down there are even paying people who have children, but no father, to help raise them! That is loco. That will never work. It encourages people to have kids to get more money from their government! It promotes bad behavior, and, of course, destroys the concept of family that God has created.

"We can see that illegitimacy rates are through the roof. One of the most powerful countries has a 40% illegitimacy rate! Why can't they see that God doesn't want them to run their lives this way? They cannot be a superpower much longer if they don't repent of this and get back to running their families the way God designed them.

"He is so kind in providing a father and a mother to nurture, care for, and raise their kids to be upstanding adults who will serve Him. If all of these kids grow up without that structure, then many of them are going to be angry and become a huge detriment to their societies in the days to come.

"It is really simple to raise kids. Now, I didn't say it is easy; I said it is simple. Just stick to the basics. Keep to what God says to do, and all the rest of it will play itself out. Even if the child goes wayward, they will have that foundation of truth which was laid in their lives to come back to. God has been so kind to give those folks the joy of parenting. We don't get to experience that, but it sure looks like fun.

"The divorce rate is out of control in some of those *enlightened* countries. They are so enlightened that they can't figure out that once they get married, they need to stay married! One of the statistics down there says that first marriages last an average of 13 years! That is crazy.

"I guess, 'Til Death Do Us Part' really meant: 'Til I Can't Stand You Anymore So I Am Not Going To Work On This or Keep My Commitment and I Am Walking Out The Door and Today We Do Part!'

"Whatever happened to people toughing things out? Whatever happened to perseverance? Why won't they follow the ways of God down there?

"And then they all talk about how great their second and third marriages are! Where is that in the Bible? I sure hope they don't see the statistics for how many people get divorced after those marriages, as well.

"We know Satan is playing around. We know he hates God and therefore hates marriage. He has been trying for millennia to convince people to throw in the towel on the covenant they made between themselves and God. People flat-out need to know how real the enemy is and what he is trying to do in their lives.

"But now, he is going for the *coup de grâce*. He is going for the complete and total destruction of the fundamental building block the Lord has given all humanity. Can you fellas believe this?"

"It is what he does. The Dean of Deception is at it again. This one is so far off the charts, I will be stunned if those people go for it. They have been so stiff-necked towards God for so many centuries, I guess it would not surprise me if they fall for this one, too," Elap reminded the others.

"Two people of the same sex being married! How can that be? That is not what God said. Do you remember when Jesus said, *'But from the beginning of the creation God made them male and female. For this cause shall a man leave his father and mother, and cleave to his wife; And they twain shall be one flesh: so then they are no more twain, but one flesh. What therefore God hath joined together, let not man put asunder'*?

"Now I am no rocket scientist here, but that cannot be any clearer, can it? That's like a window someone washed 1,000 times with Windex! You can't miss that one. As clear as a bell. Man. Woman. Marriage. Simple.

"But for a world that continues to show its hatred towards God, none of this surprises me. They have no clue what the consequences are going to be for this disobedience to Him.

"You guys remember when God had Noah, his wife, his sons, and their wives go into the Ark, correct? What was He doing? Well, we know He was showing grace to Noah because Noah walked with Him. He was God's kind of man! But God was showing those folks, once again, how important the family is as the building block of all societies. God was being the nurturer. He was being the protector. And He was demonstrating that to them. So now, all people have to do is replicate that in their lives and societies; and they will have a foundation that will not be easily broken."

"I think it might be better to force them to do that instead of giving them a choice," Onyx asserted.

"You know, God doesn't work like that," Elap reminded him. "He gives them the truth of His Word, and it is their job to obey it or not.

"You know how much the Jews love the Word of God. But many don't realize why the institution of marriage and family is the bedrock for all societies. We see examples of marriage and family sprinkled all through His Word because they are the foundations for life that He set up for all peoples! And did you know this is referred to in one of the most recited Scriptures for the Jews?

THE SHEMA

Hear, O Israel: The LORD our God is one LORD:

And thou shalt love the LORD thy God with all thine heart, and with all thy soul, and with all thy might.

And these words, which I command thee this day, shall be in thine heart:

And thou shalt teach them diligently unto thy children, and shalt talk of them when thou sittest in thine house, and when thou walkest by the way, and when thou liest down, and when thou risest up.

And thou shalt bind them for a sign upon thine hand, and they shall be as frontlets between thine eyes.

And thou shalt write them upon the posts of thy house, and on thy gates.

"God knows that in order for the family to succeed, they must know Him! They must be grounded in His Word. The number one teachers to those kids are their fathers and mothers. And He isn't talking about teaching them to brush their teeth or tie their shoes. He's talking about teaching them the Word of God! He has placed on their shoulders the massive importance of not only teaching their kids the Word, but living it out as role models before them, as well. No one else is responsible for the raising of their kids. God gives that exciting responsibility to parents, and He knows they can accomplish this task by trusting Him and doing it His way!

"He wants parents to hear Him through His Word. He wants them to listen to Him. He is showing them that He will be their protector and guide, and they must emulate that to their children, as well. That is what parents do!

"He is also warning them that if they do not take this as seriously as He is telling them they should, there will be turbulent waters ahead. There will be raging rivers of rebellion and tsunamis of trouble on the horizon if they do not follow His commands for raising their kids. It will make the waves that thrashed against the Ark seem like little ripples on a lake.

"The Ark survived those stormy times because God protected it. He's saying the same thing here. Do it His way. Follow His Word. There may be some tumultuous times up ahead for their family, but He will protect them as they lay that correct biblical foundation in their lives.

"There is really no such thing as quality time versus quantity time with God. All time is important to Him. It takes a massive amount of time to embed those biblical truths in kids' lives, but it is the best investment parents will ever make during their lifetimes!

"Remember what Paul wrote?

PARENTS AND CHILDREN

Children, obey your parents in the Lord: for this is right.

Honour thy father and mother; which is the first commandment with promise;

That it may be well with thee, *and thou mayest live long on the earth.*

And, ye fathers, provoke not your children to wrath: but bring them up in the nurture and admonition of the Lord.

"When children learn to obey their parents, they will learn to obey the Lord. Very straightforward. But if that proper biblical modeling is not there for those kids, then anything is possible. All bets are off the table. We can look down and see so many people in prisons around the world, and one of the main contributing factors is their dads did not adhere to the biblical advice that God gave them.

"From here, it's easy to understand why many of those young men are so angry. They are mad. Their dads did not spend time with them. They did not watch them play sports or go to other events they were involved in. Too busy. Chasing the almighty dollar that isn't so almighty. Divorcing their moms. And that anger would boil up. The pressure would continue to build up and build up until it exploded like a cork from a bottle. They were basically wild, untamed horses, but it didn't have to be that way. The father could have chosen not to provoke his kids. He could have chosen to spend time with his children. He could have chosen to invest in their souls. We have always known that choices have consequences, and many of those consequences are not good.

"It is like they are carrying this ball and chain around their ankles. Some of them don't even know who affixed it to them. That burden is heavy. It weighs them down. It hampers their efforts to run the race for God. I just hope those people will turn to Jesus and remember His words, *'For my yoke is easy, and my burden is light.'*

"We can see that resentment eating away at them. We can see the anger of rebellion welling up and being used to impose their will on situations. They want their way, and they are going to get it somehow. Just like witches who want to impose their will on a situation by casting a spell. They want to be in control when they are not supposed to be in control. Parents need to know that they are in control of raising their kids, and not the other way around.

"Think about if parents lived by the truth that God gave them: *'By him therefore let us offer the sacrifice of praise to God continually, that is, the fruit of our lips giving thanks to*

113

his name.' Just think if words like that were rolling off parents' lips 24/7 down there to glorify the Lord! Wow. What a sight to behold, and those words would just get infused inside of their kids' hearts and minds.

"It is so much fun to see those soul winners on the streets. Just out there having a good time talking to the lost, handing out gospel tracts, and planting seeds all over the place. When I look down, my favorite sight is seeing those dads and moms with their kids in tow out there being a bright light for the Lord in a very dark world! I was watching one time and actually saw a family out there soul winning with a baby in their stroller! I just knew they were raising their kids up to be evangelizing everywhere they go, whether they were young or whether they were old!

"We know how much God hates divorce. He hates when two people come together in a covenantal relationship with Him, and then they destroy it by parting ways. Remember when God said, *'Likewise, ye husbands, dwell with them according to knowledge, giving honour unto the wife, as unto the weaker vessel, and as being heirs together of the grace of life; that your prayers be not hindered'?* A husband's prayers can be hindered by how he treats his wife. That is strong. So can you imagine how much God hates it when a man or a woman ditches their marriage partner and walks away from them? God does not look upon that kindly.

"God just loves those long marriages. Those people sticking it out and persevering for sixty and seventy years together. What a testimony and legacy they leave for their kids and grandkids, and even for others in their neighborhoods and workplaces. They just love to see that example being set and the bar being held high. But really, the bar isn't that high. A covenant is a covenant. It is truly unbreakable from God's perspective, so it should really be unbreakable from their perspective, as well!

"A designer always gets to define their creation. God designed marriage, so He can define it! Pretty basic and straightforward.

People need to get off their high horse on this issue. If they think they know more than God does about marriage, they are sadly mistaken.

"Looking down there, though, people are not going by God's Word. People of the same sex are coming together and calling that marriage. Men are marrying more than one wife. God knows what a marriage covenant is. And they mock Him with these aberrations of His truth. They keep trying to redefine what He has already defined, but they can poke their finger in His eye only so many times until He finally has enough. I am getting the feeling those days will be coming soon.

"People need to realize that they should not lower the standard. Keep the standard high. Where do the standards come from? The Book!! It is their resource and their guide for how to live. They shouldn't drift the way the world wants them to. They should stick to God's Word.

"God wants whole households to be saved! That is His plan. Those people need to live by His plans. Remember when He said, *'But as many as received him, to them gave he power to become the sons of God, even to them that believe on his name'*? God has such big plans. He wants those people to get saved. He wants His eternal family to grow larger and larger and larger! And they get to choose. They get to decide to believe and become born again, or not. It is great seeing those big families down there, but I want to see the family of God huge up here!!

"I just wish those parents could see how important their jobs are. They are literally the leaders of the greatest team of all time! We can tell just by looking and watching people whether they had both good mommas and good daddies who raised them. Parents literally have the most important platform in the history of the world! They don't get a do-over raising their kids. What they say today might be the last thing they get to tell them. They just never know. I do hope they realize that, before it is too late."

"Wasn't it neat to see some of those folks down there upholding and modeling a strong, biblical foundation with their families?" Elap reflected back.

"Absolutely wonderful to see that during those dark days. Those last days needed to be lit up with truth and lit up brightly," Onyx agreed.

"Thankfully, some of them got the message loud and clear!" Elap said.

Chapter 16
The Long-Lasting Call

"*The Word of God is* just so powerful. We know that, but more of those folks down there need to realize its power, too. When the power of the Word is seen in its fruits, it is just so humbling to the soul. Remember when Luke wrote these words?

CASTING NETS

And it came to pass, that, as the people pressed upon him to hear the word of God, he stood by the lake of Gennesaret,

And saw two ships standing by the lake: but the fishermen were gone out of them, and were washing their nets.

And he entered into one of the ships, which was Simon's, and prayed him that he would thrust out a little from the land. And he sat down, and taught the people out of the ship.

Now when he had left speaking, he said unto Simon, Launch out into the deep, and let down your nets for a draught.

And Simon answering said unto him, Master, we have toiled all the night, and have taken nothing: nevertheless at thy word I will let down the net.

And when they had this done, they inclosed a great multitude of fishes: and their net brake.

And they beckoned unto their partners, which were in the other ship, that they should come and help them. And they came, and filled both the ships, so that they began to sink.

When Simon Peter saw it, he fell down at Jesus' knees, saying, Depart from me; for I am a sinful man, O Lord.

For he was astonished, and all that were with him, at the draught of the fishes which they had taken:

And so was also James, and John, the sons of Zebedee, which were partners with Simon. And Jesus said unto Simon, Fear not; from henceforth thou shalt catch men.

And when they had brought their ships to land, they forsook all, and followed him.

"In those times, four of the apostles were fishermen. They would fish by line, by casting out a net from land, or they would drag a net between two boats to catch fish," Ivory explained.

"Fishing for fish is one thing, but when people finally realize they are on planet Earth to fish for souls, it will move their lives up to a whole other level! It is so much fun to watch those soul winners down there! They are just flat-out going for it. And they have so many methods for how to get God's truth into the hands of the lost. It is so neat to watch their conversations with them. We can tell by their eye contact and how they listen and respond that they really do have a deep love and care for the lost.

"At other times, and especially in those mass crowds, they are handing out tracts, holding up strong biblical signs, and some are even open-air preaching. We can tell, even from this distance, which ones reach out to them in love. They sure do make the Father look good!

"It is fascinating to watch fishermen, though, who go out in their boats for those long days on the water. I like some of the qualities they have. They don't just talk about fishing; they actually go out and do it! They are productive people. They are so, so passionate about fishing. It looks like some of them would rather be on the water than anywhere else!

"Another interesting thing about fishermen is that they aren't easily sidetracked. There can be long hours of casting out their lures without a nibble, but they don't give up. Perseverance seems to be an innate characteristic in them. On-the-job training is not a bad thing! They also realize the right environments and the right conditions to fish in and invest the time necessary to get the job done.

"Now think about those qualities, and think about soul winners using those same qualities while they are out there reaching the lost. It is a process to become a great fisherman, and it is a process to become a great soul winner. Humbleness is needed for both. They both need to guard against becoming easily frustrated. Maybe that is one of the reasons why the Lord used the analogy of fishing in the Scriptures. I bet it is!

"Fishermen also know they need to go where the fish are! Doesn't do them much good to go fishing in a bathtub! They have to go to the ponds, the lakes, the streams, and the oceans. It is interesting to watch so many believers down there. They like the comfort of hanging out with other Christians in their churches and in each other's homes. Now there is a time for that, but it isn't where the lost are. The lost are on the highways and byways. They are at coffee shops, sporting events, horse races, malls, beaches, concerts, music festivals, arts and crafts festivals, parks, schools, and work places. They should be so, so excited every day to walk out of their front doors and engage those people. But I am guessing that Satan has deluded them somehow because the lost are prime for the picking. It seems like it's difficult to get some of them excited about soul winning. I don't know what they are thinking. They must have lost their eternal focus, and that is not good. They are for sure missing the boat, and that pun is intended.

"When Jesus said, *'Go ye into all the world, and preach the gospel to every creature,'* He meant it. He didn't mean for people to come up with their top ten list of why they couldn't, wouldn't, or shouldn't share their faith. He meant *get out there*. He meant *go*. He meant for people to *care about the lost and dying*.

"It is so surprising to overhear some of those conversations down there. They come up with the weakest excuses for why they won't share their faith in Jesus with the lost. Seems like so many people live with fear. Fear they won't know the right answer to a question. Fear of losing their supposed hard-earned reputation. Fear of rejection and that someone won't want to be their friend anymore. Fear of failure. Fear of thinking they are unqualified. Fear! Fear! Fear!

"The Mighty God wrote: *'And, behold, there arose a great tempest in the sea, insomuch that the ship was covered with the waves: but he was asleep. And his disciples came to him, and awoke him, saying, Lord, save us: we perish. And he saith unto them, Why are ye fearful, O ye of little faith? Then he arose, and rebuked the winds and the sea; and there was a great calm.'*

"Where is the great faith that those folks should have? Why won't they trust the Lord? He has proven Himself trustworthy over and over and over again. He knows they can trust Him. They know they can trust Him, but they don't. Simple as that.

"The words of our God are so, so appropriate: *'There is no fear in love; but perfect love casteth out fear: because fear hath torment. He that feareth is not made perfect in love.'*

"What they really need to live by is: Love! Love! Love! That is what they need. Love for the Lord. Love for the cross. Love for truth. Love for obedience. Love for each other. Love for the lost. Why don't they get it? It can be so frustrating, sometimes, seeing it from our viewpoint.

"If they are watching their televisions, playing a video game, perusing a magazine, searching a website, looking at a newspaper, or even if they are reading a book this very exact moment, why don't they put it down and read the Word of the Most High God? Read the love letter that He wrote to them? Why won't they do that? It is amazing to see how they have been so deceived. I sure wish they could see it from our perspective. They definitely would look at their time on earth in a completely different way.

"They just need to prepare themselves for battle by reading and studying the Word of God. Worshiping the Most High. Praying to God. Putting on their armor; and then, getting out there and fighting! Fishermen don't catch fish in their living rooms. They might enjoy that fishing show, but there won't be any fish in the skillet that night. They need to get up, go out that front door, and get busy. If only Christians would live by that same code of conduct, what an impact they would make!

"God's words, again, fit so perfectly here: *'So then neither is he that planteth any thing, neither he that watereth; but God that giveth the increase. Now he that planteth and he that watereth are one: and every man shall receive his own reward according to his own labour. For we are labourers together with God: ye are God's husbandry, ye are God's building.'*

"They need to get busy. They need to do their part. We know that God is going to do His part. He always does. They should already know that from reading the Scriptures and from how He has worked in their lives.

"Fishermen don't quit when they don't catch their limit each time. They get back out there the next day. They persevere. Fishers of souls need to live by the same creed.

"The Lord made it so clear for them when He said, *'Follow me, and I will make you fishers of men.'* He didn't say come follow Me, and I will make you a millionaire or a sports star or healthy all the days of your life. He has always been so straight-forward in His statements to people. It is because He cares about them. When people say 'yes' to Jesus, they say 'yes' to soul winning! Don't they understand that? That is what they are there for. That is the one thing they cannot do in Heaven. They won't be reaching lost souls up here. None around us. That is their earthly job. That is their assignment. It is either pass or fail. They either do it or they don't. They either obey Jesus, or they don't. And yet, so many of them seem to be so literally deceived on this issue.

"It would be like one thousand lifeguards celebrating a successful year of no one drowning. They are whooping it up and patting each other on the back for another successful season. Yet at the same time, the water all around their party boat is littered with people who are drowning, and they don't even realize it because they are celebrating and missing what is going on all around them. They don't throw life jackets to those drowning or lower life rafts for them. Either they can't see them, or they really just don't care. And sadly, I think number two is the answer for most of them down there.

"People's job during their days on earth is to rescue the perishing. People all around them are dying and going to Hell for all eternity, and it is like they just don't care. They won't throw them a lifeline. But if they would throw them a lifeline with the hook being the cross of the Lord Jesus Christ, there is no telling who they would catch!

"They seem to have forgotten that God used another person when they were caught! Someone talked to them about Jesus. Someone handed them a tract. Someone preached to them. Someone printed a Bible that wound up in their hands. Why won't they return the favor and do the same for someone else? How can they literally be so selfish with the eternal truth that God has placed in their hands and mouths?

"Those people need to remember what the Holy Scriptures say: *'And Jesus went about all the cities and villages, teaching in their synagogues, and preaching the gospel of the kingdom, and healing every sickness and every disease among the people. But when he saw the multitudes, he was moved with compassion on them, because they fainted, and were scattered abroad, as sheep having no shepherd. Then saith he unto his disciples, The harvest truly is plenteous, but the labourers are few; Pray ye therefore the Lord of the harvest, that he will send forth labourers into his harvest.'*

"They need to pray for more laborers to go into the harvest field of souls. But part of their prayers need to be for the one they see in the mirror. They need to have compassion for people like Jesus does. That man or woman needs to be in the harvest field. They need to get out of their comfort zone. They need to be about the Lord's work, before it is too late for them to do anything about it and too late for that lost soul who is taking their last breath without being born again. They need to rescue the perishing.

"Are those people going to burn out or rust out for the Lord? I sure wish they could see it from our angle. It is time to burn out like a Mustang laying rubber on the pavement after winning the Daytona 500!

"What they need to do is lift up the King of Glory! You remember when the Holy Spirit wrote: *'The earth is the LORD's, and the fulness thereof; the world, and they that dwell therein. For he hath founded it upon the seas, and established it upon the floods. Who shall ascend into the hill of the LORD? or who shall stand in his holy place? He that hath clean hands, and a pure heart; who hath not lifted up his soul unto vanity, nor sworn deceitfully. He shall receive the blessing from the LORD, and righteousness from the God of his salvation. This is the generation of them that seek him, that seek thy face, O Jacob. Selah. Lift up your heads, O ye gates; and be ye lift up, ye everlasting doors; and the King of glory shall come in. Who is this King of glory? The LORD strong and mighty, the LORD mighty in battle. Lift up your heads, O ye gates; even lift them up, ye everlasting doors; and the King of glory shall come in. Who is this King of glory? The LORD of hosts, he is the King of glory. Selah.'* They just need to go and tell people about the King of Glory!

"Too many people down there have that new car smell. They need to smell like fish! That fishy smell needs to be emanating from them because they spend so much time fishing for souls!

"People need to realize that each one of them is an innkeeper who decides if there is room for Jesus. There is plenty of room for Jesus in the lives of the lost. People need to let them know there is room for Him in their lives right now, and that it might literally be their last chance to be saved."

"*Those believers down there needed to take God's words to heart: 'The fruit of the righteous is a tree of life; and he that winneth souls is wise,'" Ivory declared.*

"*Thankfully, some of them did step up to tell the world about what Jesus did for them. And to see the hearts of sinners rise up to believe the Truth was a sight to behold," Onyx delighted.*

"*And the sweet praise of those who did lasted their entire lifetime! Remember those precious sounds of thanks that flowed from their lips? I can still hear it now..." Ivory savored as they moved along.*

Chapter 17
Save the Last Song for Me

"**We just love to hear** the people on earth worship the Lord from their hearts. We know they haven't seen Him yet. It will be easy for them to do that when they are up here. Even though that face-to-face encounter hasn't happened for them yet, it just seems like they have so much joy praising Him!" Crimson noticed.

"Hey, listen to that family singing together on that mountaintop."

How Great Thou Art

O Lord my God, when I in awesome wonder
Consider all the worlds thy hands have made,
I see the stars, I hear the rolling thunder,
Thy power throughout the universe displayed:

Then sings my soul, my Savior God, to thee:
How great thou art! How great thou art!
Then sings my soul, my Savior God, to thee:
How great thou art! How great thou art!

When through the woods and forest glades I wander
And hear the birds sing sweetly in the trees,
When I look down from lofty mountain grandeur,
And hear the brook and feel the gentle breeze:

And when I think that God, his Son not sparing,
Sent him to die, I scarce can take it in,
That on the cross, my burden gladly bearing,
He bled and died to take away my sin.

125

When Christ shall come with shout of acclamation
And take me home, what joy shall fill my heart!
Then I shall bow in humble adoration,
And there proclaim, My God, how great thou art!

"Oh, are they in for the shock of their lives when they finally meet Him! They have the right attitude. They are looking. They can't wait for that meeting with Him, and they will be blown away for all of eternity! *Awesome* is a word they will use forever and ever and ever!" Ivory proclaimed.

"Listen to those folks singing before they go out and hit the streets witnessing. Listen closely to those words."

Abide With Me

Abide with me; fast falls the eventide;
The darkness deepens; Lord, with me abide;
When other helpers fail and comforts flee,
Help of the helpless, oh, abide with me.

Swift to its close ebbs out life's little day;
Earth's joys grow dim, its glories pass away;
Change and decay in all around I see,
O Thou who changest not, abide with me.

I need Thy presence every passing hour;
What but Thy grace can foil the tempter's pow'r?
Who, like Thyself, my guide and stay can be?
Through cloud and sunshine, Lord, abide with me.

I fear no foe, with Thee at hand to bless;
Ills have no weight, and tears no bitterness;
Where is death's sting? Where, grave, thy victory?
I triumph still, if Thou abide with me.

Hold Thou Thy cross before my closing eyes;
Shine through the gloom and point me to the skies;
Heav'n's morning breaks, and earth's vain shadows flee;
In life, in death, O Lord, abide with me.

"We have heard people singing that hymn at funerals, but they need to sing it every time they walk out their front doors! He will abide with them every step of the way. That is what the Comforter does! He will walk with them into and through every witnessing encounter, and He will escort them to the throne of God, too! Wow!

"Now take a listen to that man in prison singing."

It Is Well With My Soul

When peace, like a river, attendeth my way,
When sorrows like sea billows roll;
Whatever my lot, Thou hast taught me to say,
It is well, it is well with my soul.

It is well with my soul,
It is well, it is well with my soul.

Though Satan should buffet, though trials should come,
Let this blest assurance control,
That Christ hath regarded my helpless estate,
And hath shed His own blood for my soul.

My sin, oh, the bliss of this glorious thought!
My sin, not in part but the whole,
Is nailed to the cross, and I bear it no more,
Praise the Lord, praise the Lord, O my soul!

For me, be it Christ, be it Christ hence to live:
If Jordan above me shall roll,
No pang shall be mine, for in death as in life
Thou wilt whisper Thy peace to my soul.

But, Lord, 'tis for Thee, for Thy coming we wait,
The sky, not the grave, is our goal;
Oh, trump of the angel! Oh, voice of the Lord!
Blessed hope, blessed rest of my soul!

And Lord, haste the day when the faith shall be sight,
The clouds be rolled back as a scroll;
The trump shall resound, and the Lord shall descend,
Even so, it is well with my soul.

"He gets it! I mean, he totally gets it! His eyes are fixed on high. He knows the Lord will take care of him inside of prison or on the outside. He knows that since Jesus died for him, He will take care of him. We can't sing that song. He didn't die for us. What beautiful words. What gorgeous words he is singing. People need to realize this, before it is too late. But there are many whose souls will not be okay. God wants everyone's soul to be at peace with Him when they die. This man in prison gets it. He absolutely gets it!

"Fellas, listen to that college girl over there. She is about to go to class and give a presentation where she is going to share her faith with her entire speech class! Listen to those words."

How Firm a Foundation

How firm a foundation, ye saints of the Lord,
Is laid for your faith in His excellent word!
What more can He say than to you He hath said,
To you who for refuge to Jesus have fled?

Fear not, I am with thee, oh, be not dismayed,
For I am thy God, and will still give thee aid;
I'll strengthen thee, help thee, and cause thee to stand,
Upheld by My gracious, omnipotent hand.

When through the deep waters I call thee to go,
The rivers of sorrow shall not overflow;
For I will be with thee thy trouble to bless,
And sanctify to thee thy deepest distress.

When through fiery trials thy pathway shall lie,
My grace, all-sufficient, shall be thy supply;
The flame shall not harm thee; I only design
Thy dross to consume and thy gold to refine.

The soul that on Jesus doth lean for repose,
I will not, I will not, desert to his foes;
That soul, though all hell should endeavor to shake,
I'll never, no never, no never forsake.

"Oh my. She is so right. He will not be forsaking her! No way on earth. Pun intended! He will use the seeds she is about to plant. Her feet are firm, and He is about to make them firmer. This will be fun to watch!

"Do you hear that beautiful sound? It is a group of homeless people under that bridge. Listen."

All Hail the Power of Jesus' Name

All hail the pow'r of Jesus' Name!
Let angels prostrate fall;
Bring forth the royal diadem,
And crown Him Lord of all!

Ye chosen seed of Israel's race,
Ye ransomed from the fall,
Hail Him Who saves you by His grace,
And crown Him Lord of all!

Let every kindred, every tribe,
On this terrestrial ball,
To Him all majesty ascribe,
And crown Him Lord of all!

Oh, that with yonder sacred throng
We at His feet may fall!
We'll join the everlasting song,
And crown Him Lord of all!

"Are they in for the time of their lives when they finally get to see Him! No more homelessness on this side!!"

"Are you listening to that man in that hospital bed?" Crimson remarked.

When I Survey the Wondrous Cross

When I survey the wondrous cross
On which the Prince of glory died,
My richest gain I count but loss,
And pour contempt on all my pride.

129

Forbid it, Lord, that I should boast,
Save in the death of Christ my God!
All the vain things that charm me most,
I sacrifice them to His blood.

See from His head, His hands, His feet,
Sorrow and love flow mingled down!
Did e'er such love and sorrow meet,
Or thorns compose so rich a crown?

Were the whole realm of nature mine,
That were a present far too small;
Love so amazing, so divine,
Demands my soul, my life, my all.

"They all are right on the money. They have come to the realization that they need to give their whole lives away to Jesus Christ. I sure hope they have more days left to do just that. Those folks down there need to realize how swiftly life rolls past them. It scoots by so quickly, and then they will meet Him. They don't get a do-over. They don't get a mulligan. They don't get a second chance. One quick life, and then a meeting with the Most High. Those people get to stand in front of Him after giving Him their all.

"It is getting close to the end now. Everyone will be meeting Him face to face soon. The time has come. He really wants to pass over their sins. He really wants them to be in Heaven. Oh, I wish those people would remember the words of *When I See the Blood*."

When I See the Blood

Christ our Redeemer died on the cross,
Died for the sinner, paid all his due;
All who receive Him need never fear,
Yes, He will pass, will pass over you.

When I see the blood, when I see the blood,
When I see the blood, I will pass, I will pass over you.

Chiefest of sinners, Jesus will save;
As He has promised, so He will do;
Oh, sinner, hear Him, trust in His Word,
Then He will pass, will pass over you.

Judgment is coming, all will be there.
Who have rejected, who have refused?
Oh, sinner, hasten, let Jesus in,
Oh, He will pass, will pass over you.

O great compassion! O boundless love!
Jesus hath power, Jesus is true;
All who believe are safe from the storm,
Oh, He will pass, will pass over you.

"Judgment Day is coming. The end is near. He will save whoever wants to be saved. Why do they reject Him? I don't think I will ever understand that."

"They write some amazing songs down there," Ivory commented.

"That is truly some great music. Listen to the melodies. Listen to the words. These might be the last hymns they ever get to sing down there. Wow."

 "We always knew truth could so impact the heart that it would cause the heart to overflow with praise and worship! Those were the songs of faith," Crimson relished.

"Of course, the equine kind has always made a lasting impression, too! Nothing else among God's creation is even in the same class. They are a sight to behold, especially when they hit their stride," Ivory declared.

Chapter 18
The Last Roundup

"*God sure did make a* lot of beautiful creatures on that remarkable planet, but I have to say I have a preference for horses! Now those are some beautiful creatures!" Crimson perked up and reflected.

"Elegant! Spirited! Majestic! Lithe! Fast! Wild! What stunning and magnificent animals.

"God's design for them is inherent in all they do. They have such a great sense of balance, which enhances their maneuverability. They can escape a situation in a moment's notice. Predators have a hard time catching them.

"Funny thing, though, horses can sleep either standing up or lying down! Now that is cool! So they can rest when they need to and be ready to go when necessary.

"Those momma horses carry their babies for nearly eleven months. And when the mare delivers the foal, the foal is ready to start running just hours after birth. Horses reach adulthood at about five years old and typically have a life expectancy of about 25 years.

"Horses also have personalities. Some of them are very high-spirited, which allows for more speed and endurance; and others are more slow and steady, which allows them to do heavy work. I've noticed there are over three hundred species of those incredible animals. Playful, strong, energetic, powerful, free, and awe-inspiring are all terms that describe those beautiful animals!

"Horses have been one of the great modes of transportation, either for long journeys, during times of warfare, or by police for crowd control. There is nothing that compares to the big, strong presence of a horse.

"They have huge eyes! They are literally nine times the size of a human eyeball. They are the largest eyes of any land animal down there. They use the upper and lower portions of their large eyes to look at things close by and at long distances. They can also see almost 360 degrees with those eyes because they are positioned on the sides of their head! This is why they always seem to be very keen to their surroundings.

"Now, humans are a funny breed! They see these beautiful horses, and the next thing they want to do is put shoes on them!! I am thinking God's hooves are just fine, but those folks on earth seem to think they can invent a better mousetrap!

"Their hooves are made of keratin, which the nails, hair, and horns of other animals are also made from. It is a very sturdy and strong material. But those horseshoes aren't a totally bad idea. They are really more like shock absorbers. So when horses are walking on streets or over rough terrain, the horseshoes absorb the shock rather than the horse's legs and joints. As we like to say, they are fancy tennis shoes! But they don't wear out as quickly as those rubber-soled ones that humans wear!!

"Some people consider the Arabian horse to be one of the most gorgeous of all land animals. It has that very unique tail and very distinctive shape to its head. This horse is amazing in its design, too, since it can literally run one hundred miles without needing rest! That is fascinating. It is one of the great endurance horses. A lot of people use this animal for show, but God has used it throughout history to glorify His name!

"Horse teeth actually occupy more space in their heads than their brains do! Probably why they enjoy a good carrot buffet so much! And they have a lot of those pearly whites. Male horses have 40 teeth, and female horses have 36 teeth.

"I know some of those basketball players down there like to play H-O-R-S-E, but you don't want to play around with a horse! Remember that old cowboy saying, 'Never approach a bull from the front, a horse from the rear, or a fool from any direction'? Don't mess with a horse!

"Gallant warriors and gentleman are known as chivalrous. What people don't know is that chivalry is derived from the word *cheval*, which is the French word for horse!

"Horses also have great memories. They don't forget anything. They remember places and situations very well. So the great thing is that when someone becomes a friend to a horse, it will never, ever forget them. Years later they can pop back up, and that horse will remember them from the past. What a great example of God's handiwork!

"The Wild West would never have been conquered without horses. The postal system was dependent upon horses. Horses hold places of great honor throughout history. And this big, strong animal actually has all four of its legs off the ground when it gallops! That is crazy to think about. We would think that a creature that big would need to be touching the ground at all points, but that is not true. Once again, this shows the design that God has put into this animal and how it will glorify Him at all times! Grace, beauty, spirit, and freedom are qualities that seem to come with a horse and its rider. Watch that horse on the open plains. He was designed for that! So graceful, so elegant with the liberty to run free. What beauty!

"Did you know that one horse down there lived to be 62 years old? They named him Methuselah in his latter years! Horses run about 27 mph, and one horse was clocked at 55 mph!!"

"Trust me. It wasn't Methuselah!" Onyx interjected.

"If I am counting correctly, it looks like to me that when we add up all of the stallions, mares, colts, fillies, ponies, broncos, foals, yearlings, geldings, mustangs, nags, and steeds, we have about 60 million of those creatures traversing planet Earth!" Crimson mused.

"There were over 1 million horses and mules killed during the Civil War, and over 8 million horses were killed during WWI. That is a lot of horses, but God graciously kept them breeding, and the earth is loaded with those marvelous creatures!

"From the Pony Express to pulling wagons, plowing, war, drawing carts, horse-drawn carriages and chariots, racing, showing, rodeo, carrying policemen, and therapeutic riding, horses have had a great career. Man O' War, Seabiscuit, Secretariat, Little Texas, Affirmed, Citation, Trigger, Buttermilk, Silver, Mister Ed, Pegasus, and Black Beauty! One thing we know for sure is that those earthly folks love horses! They even like those sea horses! I am getting the feeling that everyone down there would want a horse if they could have one!

"When someone rides a prancing horse, it is easy for them to feel like a king! Horses give a sense of confidence. There is freedom and power in riding a horse. A horse is truly one of God's great gifts to all of humanity. It is a treasure beyond measure, and what a pleasure to study this wonderful animal!

"A lot of famous folks have ridden horses, but easily one of the most famous was John Wayne. We saw people watching his movies all the time. Little did they know that Marion Morrison, John's real name, rode a horse every single day to school! He just loved Jenny. Hopped right up on top of her for another great day riding to school. He once said about riding a horse, 'Came as naturally to me as breathing.'

"But when Jenny died, it was devastating to Marion. Probably one of the reasons he never got too close to a horse again. He rode many different horses in his movies and even rode one named Duke, which was his nickname. John was a very big man, but he was very elegant and graceful on a horse. All of that riding during his younger years made him comfortable in the saddle his whole life.

"He played many different movie roles with horses; but, of course, his best role, without a shadow of a doubt, had to be

Cahill: U.S. Marshall! And I am sure most people on planet Earth would never, ever doubt that!"

"What a strange name for a movie. What is a *Cahill* anyway? Those people on earth, and probably those Cahills, sure are a funny lot!" Onyx surmised.

"This is no time for humor, Onyx!" Crimson joked as he countered back. "But interestingly, Marion Morrison was like all people on planet Earth. He took his last breath. He has now journeyed to the other side. A horse won't carry anyone there. Neither their riding skills nor their gold medals in equestrian events will matter one bit unless they have committed their life to the Creator of that gorgeous creature, the horse. God has been showing everyone the evidence of His great handiwork and workmanship through the horse. I sure hope they are not worshiping those creations more than the Creator. When we see some people treating horses better than they treat people, we know they have missed the trough.

"Horses have had a greater impact down there than people realize. Look at some of the terms they use: *stubborn as a mule, beating a dead horse, horseplay, horsing around, horse laugh,* and *a horseless carriage.* 'You can lead a horse to water, but you can't make it drink' was cited as a proverb as early as 1546. 'That's a horse of a different color' originated from Shakespeare's *Twelfth Night* in 1601. The old familiar phrase, 'Don't look a gift horse in the mouth' refers to the practice of horse traders determining the age of a horse by its anterior teeth or incisors. The incisors erupt and wear down at a fairly consistent rate throughout the life of the horse. So buyers would look inside of the horse's mouth to see how old it was! *Eating like a horse* originates from the fact that horses spend much of their time consuming large quantities of food.

"The list continues across the board with *charley horse, dark horse, front runner, give and take, hands down, home stretch, in the running, out of the running, a run for their money, running mate, wire to wire, down to the wire, upset, also ran, win by a nose, ringer, starting from scratch, chomping at the bit, heavyweight, and bits and pieces,* which are all terms that come from horse racing! They don't realize that horses have really affected how they speak and communicate. So many of those people are literally *in the home stretch* of their lives. They are *down to the wire,* but are they ready to meet the Creator of every horse they have ever seen?

"When those horses wear all of their regalia, they are really beautiful. There is something about the horse that runs free, but there is also something about those horses when they have saddles, stirrups, bridles, reins, bits, and harnesses on them. Truthfully, it seems that people need to have blinkers or blinders on themselves. They keep horses focused. They keep them from getting distracted by what is behind or to the side of them. They keep them from getting spooked. Keep them looking straight ahead. Focused on what is right in front of them, so they will be just fine. Christians need to live like that. Focused on the Lord. Kept from distractions. Reading His Word and obeying what they read. They would keep from so easily getting off track if they kept those biblical blinders on at all times.

"One thing we know for sure is that God loves horses! He created them with an especially fine touch! And their hoof prints are scattered all across the pages of Scripture.

"Now, of course, you remember all of the horses and chariots that were destroyed in the Red Sea. We see that event mentioned over and over again in the Old Testament. You guys knew what God was doing, didn't you?"

"Yes!" Ivory interjected. "He was reminding the Jews, and all people, that if He got them out of a seemingly impossible situation with the Egyptians—a situation that looked like there was no hope—He can get them out of their situation, as well. The Jews do not need to keep running away from God, but right to the God who delivered them out of slavery and out of Egypt, into the Promised Land!!

"Horses and chariots are mentioned throughout the battles in the Old Testament. They were the main mode of transportation in antiquity, and horses took warriors both into battle and out of battle. Without horses, armies would have lost many of their campaigns. Horses were how people moved around for most of history. The horse is easily one of the greatest creatures that God has ever made.

"Remember when God said, *'Woe to them that go down to Egypt for help; and stay on horses, and trust in chariots, because they are many; and in horsemen, because they are very strong; but they look not unto the Holy One of Israel, neither seek the LORD!'?*"

"Of course, I do," Crimson answered. "That is one of the problems with those humans down there. They keep relying on their own strength. How strong they are. How many horses, chariots, tanks, and guns they have. How much money they have in their bank account. All of that can help them; but in one fell swoop, God can wipe it all out. They need to put every ounce of trust they have in the Holy One of Israel. That simple. That easy. They will win every time that way. We can see it from up here, but I get the feeling that so many of them are blinded and can't see it from down there. So sad; and because of that, it will be so costly for many of them.

"The Lord lays it out so simply for them in Scripture: *'An horse is a vain thing for safety: neither shall he deliver any by his great strength. Behold, the eye of the LORD is upon them that fear him, upon them that hope in his mercy; To deliver their soul from death, and to keep them alive in famine. Our soul waiteth for the LORD: he is our help and our shield. For our heart shall rejoice in him, because we have trusted in his holy name. Let thy mercy, O LORD, be upon us, according as we hope in thee.'*

"My only guess is that they use their eyes too much. They see the strength of the horse, and they just know it will give them victory. Or they look at the caliber of their weapon and just know it is how they will win in battle. They must learn to live by faith. They must realize that the God who has created everything their eyes can see is able to get them out of a battle or a tough situation in the blink of an eye. Now that is real power! They need to start trusting Him more and more, before it is too late.

"Probably all of us have some special thoughts about Solomon. One of our favorites for sure! He had 1,400 chariots, 12,000 horsemen, and 40,000 stalls for his horses!! Now that is my kind of king!! He even had cities for his chariots and cities for his horsemen. But in spite of all that, those things were not what he trusted in. The Lord was his strength. The Lord was his Protector. No one—and no one else—could fill that position in his life.

"God is so kind in how He gives those people guidance. He told them, *'The horse is prepared against the day of battle: but safety is of the LORD.'* He is trying to warn them. He is trying to tell them to make sure they know who they should really be putting their trust in.

"Remember when God also wrote this about horses: *'Hast thou given the horse strength? hast thou clothed his neck with thunder? Canst thou make him afraid as a grasshopper? the glory of his nostrils is terrible. He paweth in the valley, and rejoiceth in his strength: he goeth on to meet the armed men. He mocketh at fear, and is not affrighted; neither turneth he back from the sword. The quiver rattleth against him, the glittering spear and the shield. He swalloweth the ground with fierceness and rage: neither believeth he that it is the sound of the trumpet. He saith among the trumpets, Ha, ha; and he smelleth the battle afar off, the thunder of the captains, and the shouting'?*

"What strong animals He has created! What power He has given them! What strength for battle He has put in them! What a presence He has given them with their nostrils and flowing manes! But that pales—and I do mean pales—Elap, in comparison to the power of the One who created them. The ultimate power is always in the power source. That power source is the Most High God who has shown His wonderful handiwork through the gorgeous creature of a horse that He has designed and made.

"God sure does love the inhabitants of earth! He also told them, *'Now know I that the LORD saveth his anointed; he will hear him from his holy heaven with the saving strength of his right hand. Some trust in chariots, and some in horses: but we will remember the name of the LORD our God.'* Horses, many times, are an example of people trusting in their carnal minds or their flesh. It might even be trusting in their tanks, their drones, or their nukes. I know it sounds like God might be repeating Himself, but we know He does that for a reason. He doesn't want them to forget. So sometimes, they need to be reminded over and over and over again of that truth. My guess is it is because they can't see Him yet. If they could, then one reminder would be enough. He knows that. He knows everything! So He lays out the truth for them, so they can understand. So loving, so powerful, and so gentle, all at the same time. His love is so amazing!

"God is so serious about those people that He loves. When He said, *'A whip for the horse, a bridle for the ass, and a rod for the fool's back,'* He meant it! There is a way to control horses and donkeys, but the wildest of the bunch tends to be humans. God also wants them under the control of His Spirit. He wants to use them mightily in these days. But too many times, they need a big wake-up call before He can get their full and complete attention.

"Y'all remember when Jesus rode into Jerusalem, don't you? It was written: *'On the next day much people that were come to the feast, when they heard that Jesus was coming to Jerusalem, Took branches of palm trees, and went forth to meet him, and cried, Hosanna: Blessed is the King of Israel that cometh in the name of the Lord. And Jesus, when he had found a young ass, sat thereon; as it is written, Fear not, daughter of Sion: behold, thy King cometh, sitting on an ass's colt.'*

"The King of Kings, the Lord of Lords, the Creator of the universe on a donkey? A domesticated animal that is used to pull heavy loads? He is a beast of burden. For the King? I just can't wrap my ears around that. If it were me, I would be arriving on an

Arabian horse, a Quarter Horse, an Appaloosa, a Thoroughbred, or a Tennessee Walking Horse! I am not arriving on some donkey or mule. But that is also why you guys know we could never be God! We are not even close to having the quality and character of Jesus. He is so humble. He is so gracious. He is so kind. He was showing these people what they were missing. They expected the Messiah to arrive in a fighter jet, and He came on a lowly donkey. So many people down there missed Him the first time, but they will not be missing Him the second time!

"There have been some famous sayings that people have come up with about horses. One famous quote is 'Riding: The art of keeping a horse between you and the ground.' Another is that famous Yiddish Proverb which says, 'The wagon rests in winter, the sleigh in summer, the horse never.'

"But the quote: 'To ride a horse is to ride the sky' will be very accurate one day. People need to look up. Their redemption is drawing nigh. *The Last Ride* is approaching. We are coming soon."

 "Horses could definitely impact a situation, but really, it was faith in the Lord that was important. He has always been the real game-changer," Ivory said.

"And right about the beginning of the 21st century, weren't we sensing that history was on the brink of something momentous? Like it was on the edge? Like a turning point of some kind was about to take place?" Crimson recalled.

"You mean like the turn in the road that we're about to make?" Ivory replied.

"Definitely. That's when things started ramping up down there. We could just tell. It was like the foundations of life that God had put in place throughout history were being set aside, and those people were giving them a last kiss goodbye!" Crimson answered.

Chapter 19
The Last Farewell

"*Can y'all tell me where* in the Bible it says that after someone goes to high school, they are supposed to go to college?" Ivory wondered.

"Now that is a strange one! First of all, you are assuming high school is mentioned in the Bible! And, of course, it is not; and we also know we don't assume things! Why are you asking that?" Onyx responded.

"Take a look. Look across the globe. People talk about this so-called *higher education*. It is the most interesting concept. I am just wondering because if it doesn't teach them about the Most High God, how can it really be a higher education?"

"Good point as always, Ivory," Onyx noted. "Satan is playing around again. He is on the move, and way too many parents—especially Christian parents—are asleep at the reins. They really need to step in and take control instead of letting their colts and fillies run wild, before it is too late. Those young people need direction as their upbringing continues. Truthfully, none of those young ones knows what they are walking into; but their parents, as their protectors and guides, should be scouting it out much more than they are.

"It is interesting to see how some of those studies say that 80% of Christian students will lose their faith during their college years, and one denomination has said that 90% of their kids will walk away from Jesus during their collegiate careers! Those statistics should make a parent cry. Those statistics should make families and churches re-evaluate *EVERYTHING* they are doing!

"What is also very interesting to see is how biblically illiterate some of those kids are. Sadly, many parents have pushed the spiritual instruction of their kids onto the church when it is their responsibility. And what they didn't know was that pizza, yo-yos, and Six Flags were going to kill those kids. If youth pastors are glorified babysitters who basically run a four-year holding tank with foosball, video games, and pizza parties, then they shouldn't be surprised with the end result that will occur. What they win them with, is what they win them to. So if they win kids to Christ with pizza, yo-yos, and Six Flags, then they will need pizza, yo-yos, and Six Flags to keep them. But if they win them with truth, then they only need truth to keep them! That worldly-type of youth-group mentality won't cut it for middle school and high school students, and it definitely won't work when they enter a college classroom.

"Why are there foosball tables, ping-pong tables, pool tables, and video games down there in those churches anyway? Don't they realize those young people get enough of that at home? They should be talking with one another. Reading their Bibles. Praying. Serving others. Helping the elderly at their church. Going and feeding the homeless. How did those churches turn out like that?

"Truth is the insurance policy against a wandering heart. The last thing they will ever need is entertainment, bands, videos, and skits. They need to know the Scriptures, solid logic, and truth. That is the prescription to make a warrior for Jesus Christ and nothing else!

"Even though studies say that young people lose their faith during their college years, I am willing to surmise that many of them really begin to walk away from the Lord and His teachings in middle school and high school. As they continue to get bombarded with the teachings and distractions of evolution, other religions, movies, phones, and video games, why wouldn't their parents think that Satan has already made a play for their hearts and their affections? He has made a move for their desires and emotions. He has made a strong play. The enemy has infiltrated the home. The barbarian himself is behind the gate, and many parents do not even realize it.

"And even worse than that, parents are the ones who have left the gate open! Not just unlocked, but wide open. They let the enemy roam around seeking whom he may devour; and sadly, the devouring is of their own children.

"If parents only knew the percentage of college professors who are professed atheists and agnostics. If parents only knew the percentage of college professors who do not believe that the Bible is the actual Word of God. If parents only knew the percentage of college professors who believe that religion does not belong in public schools. If they knew all of this, they would not send their precious offspring to sit under their teachings. They are literally sending their heirs off into the roaring lion's den. Throwing them to the wolves. That is like having them ride a bucking bronco when they have never even ridden a hobby horse or a carousel or a merry-go-round before. Not a good move, if you ask me.

"The grandest race of all down there is the Kentucky Derby! There is nothing like it. The winner has a shot at the Triple Crown. Win that race and whether you are horse or trainer, you are set up for life. People need to realize that there is an eternal life waiting for them. Judgment Day is what God wants them to get ready for. If they do not get the Crown of Rejoicing, the Crown of Righteousness, and the Crown of Glory from the Lord, it will literally go down as a wasted life. And they really do not want that to happen. And anything that cuts in on them getting these crowns needs to be questioned at all costs.

"A shallow belief system never works in the real world or in people's day-to-day lives. Doubting is okay. Asking questions is okay. Many people find answers when they start questioning. When they dig and find those answers, it will help them later when they are questioned about what they believe. If they can't answer the opposition, they begin to wonder if they really do have the right answer.

"One thing that many people wrestle with is the exclusivity of Jesus Christ as the only way to Heaven. That is pretty clear in the Scriptures. There is no wiggle room here. We know it to be true, and the Bible says it to be true. Now the question is whether those people will believe it to be true.

"Seems like the college and university system down there has so lost its mind that these classes are actually offered on campuses for actual college credit where they will actually take someone's money if they sign up for a semester of this intellectual nonsense: Whiteness: The Other Side of Racism; Alien Sex; The Textual Appeal of Tupac Shakur; The Science of Harry Potter; How To Win A Beauty Pageant; Philosophy and *Star Trek*; Tattoos in American Popular Culture; Feminist Perspectives: Politicizing Beyoncé; and Create Your Own Religion!

"That is just stunning to me. What are parents thinking when they pay for these classes? Create your own religion? Harvard was started as an institution to train up Christian ministers. Matter of fact, their motto was *Veritas Christo et Ecclesiae*, which means 'Truth for Christ and the Church.' Yale University was started when ten ministers thought Harvard had become too liberal, so they started their own college! Students who attended Yale were required to 'live religious, godly and blameless lives according to the rules of God's Word, diligently reading the Holy Scriptures, the fountain of light and truth; and constantly attend upon all the duties of religion, both in public and secret.' They were also instructed to '. . . consider the main end of his study to wit to know God in Jesus Christ' and 'to lead a Godly, sober life.' Princeton University was founded by seven ministers after the Great Awakening to train ministers and offer other fields of study, as well.

"My, how far have these colleges fallen. These universities bear no resemblance to what they were originally planned and designed for. Satan just slowly chips away; and now, these so-called institutions of higher education have literally turned into cesspools where truth is neither respected nor wanted. No wonder nations are falling by the wayside when they are hiring graduates from these universities that cannot even figure out who the Creator of the universe is! Sad times down there. These colleges will be coming to an end soon, and too many of those graduates are not ready to meet their Maker.

"I am beginning to think these indoctrination centers forgot what was in the Northwest Ordinance which was passed by the U.S. Congress: 'Religion, morality, and knowledge being necessary to good government and the happiness of mankind, schools and the means of education shall forever be encouraged.' Truth is always the first casualty of war, and truth has been lost on college campuses today.

"And not only that, but so many young people are shackled with huge debts when they leave campus. So they leave with the double whammy of false teachings being pumped into their heads and massive debt that will take years to repay. Satan sure has a stronghold on these campuses, and parents seem totally oblivious to it.

"I am not sure why those parents don't just encourage their kids to find a job or go on a mission trip to Tehran, Iran. It is a much safer place for them than a university campus in America.

"Do you remember when Luke wrote: *'Now when they saw the boldness of Peter and John, and perceived that they were unlearned and ignorant men, they marvelled; and they took knowledge of them, that they had been with Jesus'*? Luke always knew what he was talking about!"

"These false teachings circling the earth are dinosaurs," Ivory surmised. "They will one day go by the wayside when a global flood of eternal truth completely swamps over them. A lie will always die when the tsunami of truth shows up.

"When those young people down there finally take their last class, will they be ready to meet the greatest Author of the greatest Book of all time?"

"*Those training centers of the world were never what God had in mind for educating His people,*" Onyx said as they rounded the bend. *They were on the home stretch.*

"*Not even close,*" Ivory noted. "*He wanted them to learn from the King.*"

Onyx added, "*The devil knew what he was doing. He knew that exchanging lies for truth would change the world; and alas, it did.*"

Chapter 20
The Last Crusaders

"*We can tell that people* have many different views of Jesus as they are rushing towards the end of the race. Some believe he is a unique creation of God, but less than God. Some think he was a manifestation of God and a prophet. Some think he was just a wise and enlightened man. Some think he was so wise that he was able to tap into his divine consciousness or his divine Christ. Some think he was the incarnation of God. Some think he is a god, but just one of many gods. Others think he was the first creation of God and actually the archangel Michael. Others believe he preexisted as a spirit being who progressed to godhood and became the savior. Some say a great teacher. Some say an incarnation of God's love. Some say a faith healer and a miracle worker. Some say a prophet and nothing more than a prophet. Some say He was born of a virgin. Some say He was sinless. Some say He was the long-awaited Messiah, and others say he is not. Some say he didn't die on a cross, and others say He did. Some say He rose from the dead, and others say he did not. Some say He is part of the Holy Trinity, and others say there is no trinity. Some say He is God's Son, and others say God has no son," Elap elaborated.

"There sure are some interesting viewpoints of Jesus down there. We can always tell when Satan is playing around. It is really kind of easy to see from our perspective. He always tries to mess with Jesus. He always tries to get people to follow a false Jesus. He has had some success, but a true believer would not even think about budging or following his ways. Their reins are tied strongly around the Word of God, and it is their anchor. They won't be running off anytime soon, even if they get spooked. That Book has all the answers they have ever looked for!" Crimson remarked.

"But by far, the main false view of Jesus that will have major ramifications as the days run short is found in the Islamic religion. Islam will be a key player as the finish line comes into view. We can see it from afar. I sure hope the people down there can see it up close," Elap continued to observe.

"Islam holds Jesus in very high regard. The Qur'an teaches that He was virgin born by Mary. One of the legends of Islam is that when Muhammad got rid of all of the images and idols in the Ka'bah, he completely refused to destroy the image of Mary with the baby Christ.

"We can also tell that Muslims highly respect the name *Jesus,* or *Isa,* because they almost always say, 'Peace be upon him' after they recite His name. They really have an interesting reverence for Jesus, but getting close to the Truth still does not give them the truth.

"The Qur'an is clear that Jesus is a messenger of Allah, and nothing more. He is one in the long line of Islam's messengers: Adam, Noah, Abraham, Isaac, Jacob, Joseph, Moses, David, John the Baptist, Jesus, and the final prophet Muhammad.

"They also teach that Jesus was not the Son of God, and He is not God. So they do not believe in the Trinity. The Qur'an further teaches that Jesus was a wise, compassionate, and merciful teacher. The pages of the Qur'an let people know He was a miracle worker, as well.

"Believe it or not, the Qur'an also teaches that Jesus was sinless! Now, we know that to be true. We know that one for sure! But how can a final prophet be greater than a sinless Prophet?! That is a new one to us.

"Islam teaches that Jesus ascended in bodily form to Heaven, and that He shall return one day. The Qur'an says that Jesus was not crucified on the cross: someone else was put up there that *looked* like Him or bore a *resemblance* to Him. One of their traditions says it was actually Judas on the cross, who was transfigured to look like Jesus when he died.

"I am so glad we know the truth. That stuff is a bunch of malarkey. Literally, meaningless talk. If those folks had some real horse sense, they would have been able to figure this out by now. We have watched this play out from the most amazing vantage point. Jesus is God. Simple as that. There is a Holy Trinity of God the Father, God the Son, and God the Holy Ghost. Jesus died on the cross. We saw it happen! We watched it. He rose from the dead three days later. People on earth knew it happened, too. They told others about it, and then many people came out to see the resurrected Christ! For forty days He was seen publicly, so no one could miss what had just happened or who He was!

"So SIX centuries later—six hundred years later—a book comes along that tries to overturn all of that truth, and people believe it? They will believe those writings rather than eyewitness accounts of what actually occurred? This means one thing and one thing only: the Deceiver is at work. Anytime anyone tries to deny the deity of the biblical Jesus, we always see the fingerprints of Satan lurking. His hoof prints are always easy to recognize. His crazed, maniacal, evil, fiendish, and diabolical ways are actually very easy to spot: they never, ever line up with the Word of God!

"Now, at times, when he is at his scheming best, he will take those lies and move them very close to the Word of God. They will look almost like they belong next to one of the verses in the Bible. He will move his dastardly lies near the cross of Jesus, so people will think they are the truth. That is why discernment is so key as the last days wind down.

"As we can see from up here, there is an all-out war raging for the truth of who Jesus is. Jesus is God, but the Qur'an states that the religion of 'truth,' meaning Islam, will be victorious over all other religions. World domination is the goal of Islam. We watch it taking place. They make encroachments here and there as they take lands and peoples for Islam. They have what are called *bloody borders.* When an Islamic country borders up against a non-Islamic country, that border will eventually become bloody.

"One of the most barbaric ways to kill someone is to behead them. Cutting off an animal's head is not an easy thing to do. It requires ripping and cutting through a lot of muscles and bones. Doing that to a human is a slow, painful, violent death. We are not talking about a guillotine here. This is an excruciating way to die. It is a type of killing that has been used throughout history, but has gone by the wayside for many centuries. *Brutal, inhumane,* and *uncivilized* are descriptions used for this type of killing.

"Very interestingly, beheading has returned. It is on the rise again in different parts in the world. But maybe even more interesting is how common it is in the religion of Islam and basically nowhere else.

"History is a good thing to study. People can learn a lot from it. Muhammad commanded beheadings when they were raiding, looting, and killing to take territory and gain wealth. In the massacre of Banu Qurayza, Muhammad was responsible for the beheadings of almost one thousand Jewish males! He ordered all males above the age of puberty to be beheaded! So why does it surprise anyone that Muslims of today follow their leader? Their leader murdered people, so why wouldn't his true followers do the same? The answer is they do.

"When the people of earth read and study the Bible, it should not surprise anyone to read about people before the throne of God who were beheaded for their belief in Jesus and for the Word of God. Islam has shown throughout history that they hate Jews and Christians. It's like it is in their DNA. So why does it surprise anyone that Muslims are beheading people in the end of days? It's really what they should expect if they are studying history and studying their Bibles.

"The leader and founder of Islam was a soldier and a ruler. He was a caravan raider and a conqueror, and that is how he gained his wealth. The *religion of peace* did not have a peaceful beginning, and it looks like it will not have a peaceful ending either.

"The Qur'an calls for the beheading of people. It is hard to misinterpret when it says to 'smite' or 'strike their necks.' Christians and Jews are their main targets according to the Qur'an. They are the infidels. They are the unbelievers. They are believing and teaching a lie according to Islam. The destruction of Israel and the Jews are at the forefront for many followers of Islam. The Jews first and the Christians second. History has shown us this, and the end times are playing out in the same way, as well.

"Listen to what the Qur'an states. What they believe is very hard to miss once you know what they've been teaching for centuries.

"Slay the unbelievers wherever you find them..." (Surah 2:191)

"Fight those who are near you, and be harsh to them..." (Surah 9:123)

"When the sacred months are past, kill the infidels wherever you catch them..." (Surah 9:5)

"Fight the Jews and the Christians if they do not convert to Islam or refuse to pay Jizya tax..." (Surah 9:29)

"Any religion other than Islam is not acceptable..." (Surah 3:85)

"The Jews and the Christians have perverted beliefs; fight them..." (Surah 9:30)

"Maim, expel, and crucify the infidels if they criticize Islam..." (Surah 5:33)

"The infidels are unclean; do not let them into a mosque..." (Surah 9:28)

"Punish the unbelievers with garments of fire, hooked iron rods, boiling water; melt their skin and bellies..." (Surah 22:19-21)

"Behead the infidel when you catch them...Do not hanker for peace with them..." (Surah 47:4,35)

"The unbelievers are without understanding; urge the Muslims to fight them..." (Surah 8:65)

"Muslims must not take infidels as friends..." (Surah 3:28)

"Terrorize and behead the infidel, and fight them..." (Surah 8:12)

"Fight those who believe in scriptures other than the Qur'an..." (Surah 9:29)

"Muslims must muster all possible force to terrorize the infidels..." (Surah 8:60)

"How can people say that the God of the Bible and the god of Islam are the same God when the Qur'an teaches Muslims to not befriend the followers of the God of the Bible, but to kill them?! It is time for people to wake up down there, before it is too late.

"The supposed religion of peace breaks the world up into the countries where Muslims can practice their religion freely. They call these countries *Dar al-Islam*, which means 'the house of Islam.' In the countries where Muslim law is not in force and not in control, that is called *Dar-al-Harb*. That term means 'the house of war.' This is going to be a battle to the end. Islam will be a major player until the King finally returns. The teachings of Islam convey hatred for the Jews and Christians. Better to wipe them out so the house of Islam can rule the world. This is about Islamic supremacy and nothing else. Their god will rule, or there will be hell to pay. But we all know that the Most High God will have the last say. He always does!

"Why do you think the Grand Mufti of Jerusalem was so close to Heinrich Himmler and Adolph Hitler? They had the same goal. They wanted to wipe out the Jews. The Grand Mufti wanted Hitler to extend his power down into Palestine, but God never let him do that.

"The Founding Fathers of the United States of America knew the dangers of Islam. One called Muhammad a military fanatic who lived by the force of arms. He also said that the precept of the Qur'an is perpetual war against all who deny its religion. They said this religious system was evil and barbaric, and they warned about it. And now in the end of days, people are dropping their guards and accepting this religious system. This is a foolish move with time so short.

"The first war that America fought was against the Barbary pirates in the Barbary Coast War. The Barbary pirates were seizing American ships and enslaving the crews because they wouldn't pay the high taxes that the Muslims demanded. Thomas Jefferson would have none of that nonsense. That was the first military engagement approved by the United States Congress.

"And now, right towards the end, Muslims are slaughtering schoolchildren. They are kidnapping whole villages and taking the women and girls to rape and marry off to Muslim men. Many who refuse are then murdered. This political and religious system was rotten at the beginning and is rotten to its core at the end.

"And during many of these killings, the perpetrators shout *Allahu Akbar*, which can be translated 'God is great,' 'God is greatest,' or 'God is greater.' What they are saying is our god is greater than your God, and we will prove it. We will kill you to show you that. We will take over your lands and your territories and show you who has the real power.

"Of course, they keep forgetting that there is another side. They keep forgetting there is a Judgment Day. They keep forgetting they will be meeting the Most High God one day. He will let them know Who is the greatest, and no murder of the innocent will be necessary to prove it!

"The threat of Islam has always been present from the beginning of its devious inception until now. We have seen it. We have observed it. We have witnessed it literally destroy civilizations.

"Y'all remember when John Quincy Adams said, 'The natural hatred of the Mussulmen (Muslims) towards the infidels is in just accordance with the precepts of the Koran…The fundamental doctrine of the Christian religion is the extirpation of hatred from the human heart. It forbids the exercise of it, even towards enemies… In the 7th century of the Christian era, a wandering Arab…spread desolation and delusion over an extensive portion of the earth… He declared undistinguishing and exterminating war as a part of his religion…The essence of his doctrine was violence and lust, to exalt the brutal over the spiritual part of human nature'?

"Adams again said, 'The precept of the Koran is perpetual war against all who deny that Mahomet is the prophet of God. The vanquished may purchase their lives, by the payment of tribute; the victorious may be appeased by a false and delusive promise of peace; and the faithful follower of the prophet may submit to the imperious necessities of defeat: but the command to propagate the Moslem creed by the sword is always obligatory, when it can be made effective. The commands of the prophet may be performed alike, by fraud, or by force.'

"He also said, 'I have made it a practice for several years to read the Bible through in the course of every year. I usually devote to this reading the first hour after I rise every morning.' No wonder he had such passion. No wonder he was one of the leaders to end slavery. He washed his mind with the Word of God, and it literally infused his mind and his soul with truth.

"Do you remember when Winston Churchill said, 'But the Mahommedan religion increases, instead of lessening, the fury of intolerance. It was originally propagated by the sword, and ever since, its votaries have been subject, above the people of all other creeds, to this form of madness . . . In each case civilization is confronted with militant Mahommedanism. The forces of progress clash with those of reaction. The religion of blood and war is face to face with that of peace. Luckily the religion of peace is usually the better armed'? He knew. He knew that the final outcome of this religious system would be its attempt at total conquest of all other religions and their territories.

"He also knew that the religion of peace was Christianity, no matter what anyone is saying these days. The Prince of Peace brings peace, and the religion of Islam brings war and has always brought war.

"You guys remember when Teddy Roosevelt said, 'Christianity is not the creed of Asia and Africa at this moment solely because the seventh century Christians of Asia and Africa had trained themselves not to fight, whereas the Moslems were trained to fight. Christianity was saved in Europe solely because the peoples of Europe fought. If the peoples of Europe in the seventh and eighth centuries, and on up to and including the seventeenth century, had not possessed a military equality with, and gradually a growing superiority over the Mohammedans who invaded Europe, Europe would at this moment be Mohammedan and the Christian religion would be exterminated. Wherever the Mohammedans have had complete sway, wherever the Christians have been unable to resist them by the sword, Christianity has ultimately disappeared. From the hammer of Charles Martel to the sword of Sobieski, Christianity owed its safety in Europe to the fact that it was able to show that it could and would fight as well as the Mohammedan aggressor . . . The civilization of Europe, America and Australia exists today at all only because of the victories of civilized man over the enemies of civilization because of victories through the centuries from Charles Martel in the eighth century and those of John Sobieski in the seventeenth century. During the thousand years that included the careers of the Frankish soldier and the Polish king, the Christians of Asia and Africa proved unable to wage successful war with the Moslem conquerors; and in consequence Christianity practically vanished from the two continents; and today, nobody can find in them any *social values* whatever, in the sense in which we use the words, so far as the sphere of Mohammedan influences are concerned. There are such *social values* today in Europe, America, and Australia only because during those thousand years, the Christians of Europe possessed the warlike power to do what the Christians of Asia and Africa had failed to do—that is, to beat back the Moslem invader.'

"Teddy Roosevelt knew there was a time for peace and a time for war. Peace is always better. Much more fun to live under those circumstances. But if someone is trying to destroy your way of life or your life, it is a time to stand against those people. You are defending the people around you and the lives of future generations to come. Their lives are worth defending, and defending does mean to the death sometimes. God will always have His remnant at all times. Satan may try and use this religious system to wipe out that remnant, but he will fail like he always does.

"Islam has one overarching goal. It is to contain, then conquer, and finally to eliminate and destroy all other religions. Once you know their ultimate goal, it is easy to see how their day-to-day operations are accomplishing it. But if Christians would reach Muslims, day by day, with the truth of the real Jesus, it could stop that false view of God in its tracks.

"Islam has always been spread by the sword, from its beginning until now at the end. Not true in biblical Christianity. You cannot find even one act in the life of Jesus that compares to any of the violence Muhammad perpetrated. Comparing these two is like comparing a Clydesdale to a Shetland pony. There is truly no comparison. Even that comparison doesn't do justice to their differences. Truly no one—and nothing—compares to Jesus.

"Muhammad claimed that he was taken by a white-winged horse of fire to Heaven! He said that the horse's name was *Burak*, and it was presented to him by the archangel Gabriel. Only one problem: It never happened! Just another fabrication by someone trying to steal the place of Jesus on a white horse. Sadly, they will meet the real Rider one day very soon, and they are not ready for that meeting. They are playing a game they are going to lose.

"Muslims believe a final ruler will come on the scene called the *Mahdi*. But interestingly, he will have a sidekick: Yes, Jesus! But if that does play itself out, it will be a false Jesus who will lie to the people. He is supposed to tell the people that he is not god, he did not die on the cross, and he did not rise from the dead. People on earth need to know that if they ever see that occur, it will not be the Jesus of the Bible, but someone literally inspired by the devil. I do hope they won't be deceived into following a lie like that.

"They say the Mahdi will come to Jerusalem riding on a white horse. Here we go again! He should have surrendered his life to the real Rider of the real white horse. This won't end well for him.

"It is interesting that the beginning of Christianity began with love: *'For God so loved the world, that he gave his only begotten Son, that whosoever believeth in him should not perish, but have everlasting life.'* Christianity will last forever in the same way it started: Love. God loved them enough to visit them, die for them, resurrect for them, prepare an eternal home for them, and make one final return for them. Love! Love! Love! Islam began with a mass murderer. Muhammad killed people. Plain and simple. And now, the last curtain call is coming to a close with that same group murdering, just like its founder did.

"People need to stand against this false teaching. People sometimes need to put their hooves down and not budge. They know what truth is. They need to stand up for it, and share it with others. The love, truth, and compassion of Jesus will always trump the lies and murders of Islam. Will they or won't they make that last stand for the biblical Jesus? Only time will tell, but time is running out."

"Truth would have made all the difference in the world to those who were caught up in the lies of Islam. Too many naysayers who followed that religion insisted on denying the truth which was right before their eyes. No wonder it was the last of days," Elap declared.

"Let's keep moving, fellas. We're almost there. Remembering these things gets my blood pumping and my nostrils snorting," Crimson said, doing some headshaking.

Chapter 21
The Last Affair

"We know the days have to be running short down there. All we have to do is look at the church—not the world—and realize that God will not put up with this much longer," Onyx surmised.

"False teachings are running rampant, and corralling them won't be easy. If the pasture isn't watered by the Word of God, it won't be green anywhere. Lies are wafting in the air. Their ears are being tickled. The fetters of truth are being bucked off to let their hearts run free. And they seem to love it that way! They need to be dusting off their Bibles and reading them instead.

"You recall when Paul was speaking to the Bereans. That was some good preaching! Remember when *'they received the word with all readiness of mind, and searched the scriptures daily, whether those things were so'*? Here was the famous Apostle Paul coming through town. If there was one person they could trust, it was him! *Nope* is what the Bereans said! They knew the frailties of human beings. They knew that people like to be liked too much. Pleasing other people can literally cloud one's judgment. Some of those pastors down there can start off on the right hoof and then get off track so easily by wanting everyone to like them.

"Truth doesn't worry about things like that. Truth is truth. Truth needs to be preached whether people like them or throw them in the lion's den. It is as simple and as truthful as that.

"I wish those people would just live by TETE: Test Everything and Test Everybody. If they would test everything they read and hear and everybody they listen to against the Word of God, they would be much better off in the finals days of planet Earth.

"Remember when Solomon wrote: *'The simple believeth every word: but the prudent man looketh well to his going'?* They shouldn't believe every wind of doctrine out there. That would make them a simple-minded person. No one would want that moniker. Test. Test. Test. Then they will be just fine.

"We see leaders, but some of them are leading people in the wrong direction—away from truth. Away from the Lord and towards sin. They are teaching a different way to live. They are teaching different gospels. We heard Paul warn them, *'I marvel that ye are so soon removed from him that called you into the grace of Christ unto another gospel: Which is not another; but there be some that trouble you, and would pervert the gospel of Christ. But though we, or an angel from heaven, preach any other gospel unto you than that which we have preached unto you, let him be accursed. As we said before, so say I now again, if any man preach any other gospel unto you than that ye have received, let him be accursed.'* The evil one wants everyone to bear with his lies.

"It's hard to believe that some of those pastors are preaching a false prosperity gospel. Come to Jesus and get stuff. What is that all about? Getting material things is not a sign of godliness. A lot of people in the world have gained wealth, and most of them will never have anything to do with the Lord! So why would any Christian think that way?

"The two main reasons people must have bought that lie are probably because their flesh likes material things, and they keep trusting their pastors implicitly. If they would just trust the Word of God implicitly, they would be in a much, much better position.

"All they need to do is look at Scripture where God wrote: *'But godliness with contentment is great gain. For we brought nothing into this world, and it is certain we can carry nothing out. And having food and raiment let us be therewith content. But they that will be rich fall into temptation and a snare, and into many foolish and hurtful lusts, which drown men in destruction and perdition. For the love of money is the root of all evil: which while some coveted after, they have erred from the faith, and pierced them-selves through with many sorrows.'* Keep it uncomplicated. Live a godly life. Live a holy life. Live a humble life. This is well-pleasing to the Lord. Wealth is literally a snare that has trapped so many people, yet they think it is something they should be striving after!

"What they should be praying for is a heart to handle wealth if it shows up on their doorsteps. God blesses so many people on Earth. He can get the funds to them, but can He get those funds through them to do His work and to support soul winning in their towns and elsewhere? That is the real question.

"Remember when Jesus said, *'Take heed, and beware of covetousness: for a man's life consisteth not in the abundance of the things which he possesseth'*? I would call that pretty clear where I come from! But things are pretty clear up here. Very clear, really. I guess it can get foggy down there sometimes.

"Or when the Lord inspired David to write: *'A little that a righteous man hath is better than the riches of many wicked. For the arms of the wicked shall be broken: but the LORD upholdeth the righteous.'* A lot of heartache for them, especially when they twist the Word of God to go after ungodly gain.

"One thing we can see from up here is something called the Charismatic Movement. Now, what is interesting is that God has instructed people to go by His Word and His Word alone. It's all they need to lead a wonderful, God-fearing life. But I guess because of the fleshly nature of humans, they seem to migrate towards things that touch or feed the flesh instead of the spirit. That can be a very dangerous journey. Satan is always after the flesh. If he can get to someone's flesh, it is much easier to gain their spirit.

"One of those inroads is the speaking in tongues phenome-non, which has really taken off among the churches. The Azusa Street movement started the explosion of tongues during the 20th century. And then, when some big-name preachers embraced it, it really began to spread. Now it is literally crossing all denom-inational lines.

"What is interesting, though, when we watched the book of Acts play itself out, is that speaking in other tongues was speaking in another known language. It was not this babbling we see those people messing around with. That is not biblical tongues. All they would have to do is read the book of Acts and 1 Corinthians, and it would become very clear to them.

"But it sure seems to be one of the biggest movements down there. That is where the money is. As one guy said, 'The true gospel is funded by nickels and dimes, but the tongues movement is funded by literally millions of dollars.' It is what we mostly see over the airwaves down there, so it's easy to tell how it ties back to the prosperity gospel. As they always say, follow the money! When people do that, they can find out rather quickly what is really going on.

"It has now led people to teach that if one doesn't speak in tongues, they are not saved! They say tongues are the evidence of the Holy Spirit working in their life. Of course, that is not what Galatians 5 teaches, but that is why Satan is the deceiver. Displaying the fruits of the Spirit should be enough for anyone who lives on planet Earth.

"In a biblical sense, *tongues* refers to a spoken and known language. It is not some kind of ecstatic speech or unintelligible gibberish. It was truly miraculous at Pentecost to see people speak in a language they didn't even know! What a grand miracle from the Lord to hear them speak about the wonderful works of God! And lost people were always present when believers were speaking in tongues. Why? God wants people to hear the gospel. God wants people saved. God wants people to repent and believe. He is that passionate about reaching the lost, and Christians need to be that passionate, as well.

"And probably, the most interesting thing is that false tongues are spoken by Satanists! The Hindu cults have ecstatic babbling as part of their rituals. Witch doctors in Africa and practitioners of Voodoo do the exact same things. Kundalini Yoga and the Shakers have these exact same utterances. That should make everyone pause. If they are making the exact same sounds, then people should immediately question the spiritual source from whence they come.

"There seems to be another phenomenon going around that during worship services, gold dust will fall from the ceiling and put a light coating of gold dust on people's hands, hair, and shoulders. So this has to be from God, doesn't it?

"That is not the most discerning group down there! Where in the Bible does that ever happen? Jesus sure did a lot of miracles, but He definitely didn't do the fishes and loaves with a side of gold dust! It almost seems like these people believe that any manifestation that happens has to be from God. Are they not forgetting that the great Deceiver himself is actively working to lure many into Hell and to lure believers into false teachings?

"Another amazing teaching taking place is that people can be physically healed—and should be physically healed—all the time. That true believers do not entertain sickness. It is not part of their walk with God. That is so far from the truth. Their sins are healed and washed away by His blood, but their flesh will always have issues in a fallen world. It also looks like death is a pretty bad sickness! And since everyone down there is dying, I guess they won't be avoiding sickness after all!

"It is amazing to watch people be so deceived by trickery. Those false miracles, which are propagated as a sign from God, are some of the saddest things we witness. The horseplay being used to deceive people is beyond the pale. No pun intended, Elap!"

"None taken!" Elap replied.

Onyx continued, "Watching those fake healings really sickens me. They bring glory to the person doing the ministering and not to the Lord. That should be an obvious giveaway. Also, if what they are doing is truly of God, why don't they visit the nearest hospital and just go room to room healing people? The reason is they can't do it! They can't heal those people. It's nothing more than deception to ultimately get money out of someone's pocket. Sad, sad days down there.

"Those people sure are an accepting lot. It's like they will almost take anything as gospel truth without testing it. Dreams, signs, and visions are taken carte blanche. They have to be true, and we don't have to test them. That is one of the most dangerous things we have ever seen. The angel of light is desperately deceiving again to destroy the lives of believers. They have the true Word of God in their hands. They need to test everything by that book, and it seems like many of them don't want to do that.

"God has specifically instructed them in His Word to *not* look for signs and wonders. They are supposed to walk by faith and not by sight. God has seemingly made it so basic for them, but they are really a wandering group.

"Have you also noticed that when someone questions the dreams or signs they claim to have received, many seem offended? Like you are actually questioning God? He is the One who told people to test things against His Word! There is not going to be any new revelation added to the canon of Scripture after the book of Revelation. They need to be much more discerning, before it is way too late.

"Another shocking practice we see is found in this *slain in the spirit* movement. Someone puts their hand near or on the forehead or chest of someone else, and that person falls backward to the ground. It is like they swoon or faint as they *come under the power*. When this spirit hits them, it can also lead to uncontrollable laughter or even barking like dogs. Only one small problem: That can't be found anywhere between the pages of Genesis and Revelation! This is anathema to God. People having this uncontrollable laughter as souls go to a lake of fire for eternity. Disgusting. It is not the Holy Spirit doing this, but a totally foreign spirit. And we know who that is, but I can't figure out why those folks don't know who it is, too.

"Also, what is so interesting is that the Bible does talk about falling backwards at different times. When it occurs, it is the judgment of God! It is not done in the sense that the Holy Spirit just hit me with some divine power. No. They are going against God's Word, and He is bringing judgment.

"And we are also seeing in the Charismatic Movement that women are allowed to be preachers. God absolutely forbids that. A pastor is to be the husband of one wife. There are not co-pastors in the Bible. Men are supposed to be the spiritual teachers, and women are not to have spiritual authority over men. It says right in God's Holy Writ that Adam was created first, and Eve was deceived. That is one of the reasons why God has established this order in spiritual matters, as well.

"As we can see, the feminist movement is moving at a very rapid pace down there. It has now infiltrated the church. Feminists have misled people into thinking that if a woman cannot be a pastor, the church is treating her as less than a man. That is far from biblical truth. God has given different roles to different people. It's literally that straightforward. If people would follow the roles God has designed for them, their lives would be so much less complicated. If they keep trying to do what God has not created them to do, then frustration will be their fruit in the coming days.

"What is also obvious, from our perspective, is the Charismatic movement is going to be used along with the ecumenical movement to bring false churches together under one umbrella. This is dangerous, and this is unbiblical. God has given them guidelines to live by, and they need to just follow them.

"Do you remember when Amos wrote: *'Can two walk together, except they be agreed?'* People cannot be walking two different paths when it comes to doctrine. They will eventually split and walk apart from one another. People need to be in agreement with God's Word instead of trying to get God's Word to come into agreement with what they want. It would be much simpler to do it God's way instead of their way.

"But those people tend to unify under leaders rather than under correct doctrine. Seeing the deification of man and some pastors has been stunning to watch, as well. It is so interesting to watch certain preachers try and fill up stadiums so their ministries can grow larger.

"From our perspective, history has literally been littered with men of God who were put on pedestals and then tumbled to the ground later. They enjoyed being on that pedestal. They enjoyed the big crowds. They took to heart the pats on their backs, which fed their egos. And all the while it was setting them up for a great fall. Only the Lord belongs on a pedestal. That is as clear as it gets. Men of God need to realize that if they ever get put up on a pedestal, they need to humbly step off of it, or God will be knocking them off of it one day. It is His pedestal. No one else belongs on it.

"The words of God again come into play here as they always do: *'Love not the world, neither the things that are in the world. If any man love the world, the love of the Father is not in him. For all that is in the world, the lust of the flesh, and the lust of the eyes, and the pride of life, is not of the Father, but is of the world. And the world passeth away, and the lust thereof: but he that doeth the will of God abideth for ever.'* Again: very simple. Money temptations, sexual temptations, and pride temptations are always what bring down men of God. They need to guard their hearts against the wiles of the devil. Those were the same lusts he used in the Garden, and those are the same tricks he is using now.

"It's like that pastor who used a marketing survey in the neighborhoods around his church to find out what people wanted in a church. That is one of the most amazing things we have ever seen! Why would he ask lost people what they wanted in a church? The answer is always in the Scriptures for things like that.

"Church is for saved people! Church is for corporate worship of the Lord. Church is for good, solid biblical preaching. Church is for biblical truth. Church is for being equipped to be soldiers for the Lord Jesus Christ who will reach the lost. Church is not a social club. It's stunning, from this viewpoint, to see how many people do not take those commands seriously enough.

"We wonder, though, if some of those pastors have dollar signs in their eyes. They know that the more people who come through the door, the more money will come in. All they would have to do is read the Word of God to know that God just loves blessing His followers. We have seen it all through history.

"One very sad thing we see is people challenging the Word of God. What utter foolishness. God's Word has stood the test of time, but man's words have not. They have fallen into the dustbins and troughs of history, but God's words stand tall!

"Why won't they listen to Peter when he wrote: *'For all flesh is as grass, and all the glory of man as the flower of grass. The grass withereth, and the flower thereof falleth away: But the word of the Lord endureth for ever. And this is the word which by the gospel is preached unto you'*? But I guess they won't follow His words because they don't believe those words.

"Again, this is very uncomplicated. Either they will let God's Word judge them, or they will set themselves up in judgment over God's words. That is a dangerous, dangerous place to be. It is a humble spirit that will do the former, and it is an arrogant spirit that will do the latter.

"As the Holy Spirit guides them into all truth, the Bible is not that difficult to understand. They need to read verses in context. They should let the clear verses help them interpret the less clear ones. As they do, then they all begin to fit together in a beautiful mosaic that glorifies the cross of Jesus! But when people want to sit in judgment of God's Word and want it to mean what they want it to mean, then trouble is on the horizon. For so many of them, it is because they want people to like them. They want sinners to like them. They want to go with the flow of the world instead of with the Word of God. Whichever way the winds of the world blow, that is the way they will follow. They want to keep peace. They want to be accepted by the people in their city. They are literally fools who are not thinking about the journey they will be making to the other side.

"For instance, look at the issue of gay marriage. There is a zero percent chance that anyone, let alone a follower of Jesus, could read the Bible front to back and get gay marriage out of that book. No way on earth! Oh wait. I guess it is *yes way* on earth!

169

"When Jesus speaks, people need to listen carefully. When He said, *'But from the beginning of the creation God made them male and female. For this cause shall a man leave his father and mother, and cleave to his wife; And they twain shall be one flesh: so then they are no more twain, but one flesh,'* He meant what He said. One man and one woman in marriage, and there are no other options.

"I can totally see how the world can mess this up. When they are led by Lucifer, the god of that world, anything is possible. But Christians? Pastors teaching this in their pulpits and saying it lines up with the Word of God? How can that be?

"The only possible answers are they are putting themselves above the Word of God, or they really want worldly sinners to like them. Some of them, I guess, don't want to hurt anyone's feelings. The funny thing is that truth doesn't come down to feelings. It comes down to truth! Right is right, and wrong is wrong. Do you remember when Isaiah penned: *'Woe unto them that call evil good, and good evil; that put darkness for light, and light for darkness; that put bitter for sweet, and sweet for bitter! Woe unto them that are wise in their own eyes, and prudent in their own sight!'?* He literally must have been talking about this generation and didn't even know it!

"Some people down there even reject the notion of an eternal Hell. I can totally understand why they don't want there to be one, but belief doesn't override reality. There is a hell. People are going there. Many are on a fast track to get there, and it is like they are living without a care in the world. They are in a speeding Ferrari with a little prancing horse on the front. They think they have it made. They are alive today, they have money in their pocket, and their sports team just won the big game. What they don't realize is that the Ferrari is heading over a cliff at warp speed. They go from being born to a cemetery at lightning-quick speed. Why don't they search to find out what is waiting for them once they head off the cliff into eternity?

"God is a holy God. He will judge the wicked. All people on the face of the earth have broken the laws of God. It is pretty easy to see that from up here. A *good person* is such a relative term. People might think they are good down there, but there are only two categories on the other side: lost and saved. That's it. He made it pretty simple. They have sinned, and God provided a Savior. Now it is their choice to decide what to do with Him.

"God is not playing games here. He is an eternal Being, and all of the humans He has created are eternal, as well. They will live somewhere forever and ever and ever. Hell, in the Bible, is described as everlasting fire, unquenchable fire, shame and everlasting contempt, everlasting destruction, and torment with fire and brimstone. Does this sound like a game?

"This is serious business, and folks down there treat it like child's play. Satan has so tricked lost people. Hell is supposed to be for the devil and his angels. People are not supposed to go there. God has given them a way out through His One and Only Son, but they must repent and believe. So simple. Get up and get moving on the narrow road. Now. Before it is too late.

"For the life of me, though, I can't figure out how Christians can claim to be Christians and not think there is a hell. The Scriptures are clear. The trickster must have gotten to them, too, somehow. Seems like Satan is playing chess while some of those Christians are playing checkers. He has seriously clouded their judgment. God's Word is clear.

"You remember when the rich man in Hell said, *'have mercy on me, and send Lazarus, that he may dip the tip of his finger in water, and cool my tongue; for I am tormented in this flame.'* He was not joking. He knows Hell is hot, and he knows it is eternal. Will those believers wake up, before time runs out, and stop people from going to that place?

"I guess one other really false teaching that takes the cake is *universal reconciliation*, which is the belief that everyone will one day make it to Heaven. We see lost people playing around with that false doctrine. They think a good God wouldn't put anyone in Hell. They, of course, forget His holy side and His wrathful side. But Christians believing that?

"In two of the best-selling books down there, the authors believe in universal reconciliation. One author has even said he believes that sometime in eternity future all people who end up in Hell, all angels who end up in Hell, and even Satan himself will one day exit Hell, go through the blood of Jesus Christ, and enter into glory in the heavenlies. Only one problem: That isn't in the Bible! Just another teaching created by men who twist the Scriptures to their own destruction.

"Let's see what the Creator of Heaven and Hell had to say about getting to the right eternal destination:

THE HOPE OF SALVATION

Who will have all men to be saved, and to come unto the knowledge of the truth.

For there is one God, and one mediator between God and men, the man Christ Jesus;

Who gave himself a ransom for all, to be testified in due time.

~

Neither is there salvation in any other: for there is none other name under heaven given among men, whereby we must be saved.

~

He that believeth on the Son hath everlasting life: and he that believeth not the Son shall not see life; but the wrath of God abideth on him.

~

That if thou shalt confess with thy mouth the Lord Jesus, and shalt believe in thine heart that God hath raised him from the dead, thou shalt be saved.

For with the heart man believeth unto righteousness; and with the mouth confession is made unto salvation.

For the scripture saith, Whosoever believeth on him shall not be ashamed.

For there is no difference between the Jew and the Greek: for the same Lord over all is rich unto all that call upon him.

For whosoever shall call upon the name of the Lord shall be saved.

Onyx continued, "And just to make sure no one could get this wrong, Jesus Himself said, *'I am the way, the truth, and the life: no man cometh unto the Father, but by me.'* Simple. Straightforward. True.

"You couldn't get many paths to Heaven, or universal reconciliation, out of that Book if you tried. But Satan is trying to deceive, and people are believing the deceiver instead of the Eternal Truth Giver.

"And now rearing its ugly head again is the teaching that God preselects who goes to Heaven and preselects who goes to Hell. What is up with that? God has always given men and women free will. They have always had the ability and responsibility to make choices. They will make good ones and they will make bad ones, and they will live with the consequences. Some of their choices will most definitely have eternal consequences, and they will live with those forever.

"Adam and Eve had a choice to either eat of the fruit of the tree of the knowledge of good and evil or to obey God and not eat of that tree. They, of course, failed miserably, and the consequences of their decision remain to this day.

"God did not force them to eat from the forbidden tree. That is not His character. He allowed them to make choices under His beautiful sovereignty. He is God. There is none other, and He allows people to choose.

"Judas chose to betray Jesus, and he suffered major consequences because of that choice.

"The rich man in Hell was not complaining that God consigned him to Hell or that he had no choice but to go there. He knew he made the terrible decision to reject God's mercy and love. He knew it was his own fault. He also wanted his brothers to be warned so they would not come to that place of torment. He knew for a fact that God hadn't preselected his brothers to go to Hell. Both he and God wanted them to repent and believe upon the Lord Jesus Christ.

"I also cannot figure out what Bible those people are reading. God sure does make Himself crystal clear on this topic. Look what Peter wrote: *'The Lord is not slack concerning his promise, as some men count slackness; but is longsuffering to us-ward, not willing that any should perish, but that all should come to repentance.'*

"How about Luke, when he wrote: *'Likewise, I say unto you, there is joy in the presence of the angels of God over one sinner that repenteth.'*

"But there is more proof that man chooses to repent and believe in the Word of God. The more you read it, the more it crystallizes truth. Joel wrote: *'And rend your heart, and not your garments, and turn unto the LORD your God: for he is gracious and merciful, slow to anger, and of great kindness, and repenteth him of the evil.'*

"Or how about when Isaiah wrote: *'And therefore will the LORD wait, that he may be gracious unto you, and therefore will he be exalted, that he may have mercy upon you: for the LORD is a God of judgment: blessed are all they that wait for him.'*

"And as Jeremiah added: *'If so be they will hearken, and turn every man from his evil way, that I may repent me of the evil, which I purpose to do unto them because of the evil of their doings.'*

"This is so clear. God didn't want anyone to miss this. His loving, gracious character wants everyone to be saved. *EVERYONE.* Not a certain select few. *EVERYONE.* His atoning work for the sins of those people is for everyone down there. Don't they get it?

"My only guess is that Satan has literally deceived some of them into not reading their Bibles with the character of the Most High God in mind. Once they know His character, His Word should be easy for them to understand.

"It seems obvious that many of these people are not getting this teaching from the Bible. They are reading all these other books. They are listening to popular speakers. They are forgetting to test them by the Word of God. That's when Satan sinks a hook in them and begins the reeling process. And then they are carried so far away from the truths of God's Word that they literally don't even know it. It is so sad to watch that happen to so many of them.

"This is as clear as clear can be! Literally, crystal clear. We have some things up here that are so pure that they are going to wonder why they called anything transparent glass!!

"And if all of that isn't enough, the visible church has now allowed ancient mystical practices into their churches and congregants' lives. These practices are putting people into altered states of consciousness, which they call *the silence*. The only problem is these are taken from the occult! I guess that is no big deal to some people in those churches. But we can see what they are doing, and we can see how deceived they really are. What they are doing is taking those occultic practices and wrapping them in Christian terminology, and that is how Lucifer is deceiving so many people.

"One of their goals is to convince people that 'God is all' or 'God is in all' or 'the universe is an extension of God.' The terms they use are *pantheism* and *panentheism*. Only one small problem: That is not the God of the Bible!! Pretty simple, don't you think?

"Folks down there seem to be so easily deceived. God tells them one thing, and they go running off to do something else or believe something else. I know they can't see Him yet; but they should know enough by now to cozy up to His Word, meditate on those scriptures, study to show themselves approved unto God, obey what they read, and then watch God use them big time in the dark days they are living in.

"These mystical practices end up trying to empty oneself by emptying the mind. They focus on nothing. They want to just *be*. But the Scriptures say to meditate on God's Word both day and night.

"Or sometimes they teach them to do breath prayers, chanting, or mantras. They use the terms like *spiritual formation*, *spiritual disciplines*, *ancient/future*, *centering prayers*, or *labyrinths*. These are the doorknobs they turn to open the doors to this type of mysticism. Collectively, they call such practices *Contemplative Spirituality*. Where are these in the Scriptures?

"Of course, they aren't there. These practices cause them to have subjective experiences that they think are from God. Then the danger is elevating these subjective, mystical experiences over the Word of God.

"Another thing that happens is that they don't realize they are playing with demons! When they open themselves up to otherworldly experiences, it's like posting a 'We Are Open' sign to every demon out there to come and play around. Again, it is not a playground but a battleground down there.

"Never forget what Joshua wrote: *'This book of the law shall not depart out of thy mouth; but thou shalt meditate therein day and night, that thou mayest observe to do according to all that is written therein: for then thou shalt make thy way prosperous, and then thou shalt have good success. Have not I commanded thee? Be strong and of a good courage; be not afraid, neither be thou dismayed: for the LORD thy God is with thee whithersoever thou goest.'* People need to meditate on God's Word. That is biblical! People need to renew their minds daily by soaking them in the truths of God's Word. All of those other types of meditation are never found on the pages of Holy Writ."

"Have you noticed what I've noticed down there?" Elap said.

"People are using the same kind of music that the world uses in their churches, conferences, and worship experiences for the Lord. Why would they do that? I wonder if they realize how powerful music really is?"

"Elap, have you taken a few laps around the globe and are seeing things? Or maybe someone confused Elap with email, hacked your account, and is sending you hoax emails! Those people wouldn't dream of doing that, would they?" Onyx said in disbelief.

"The only thing I'm seeing here are the words of Daniel, and he can give us some great insight," Elap replied. "Remember when he wrote: *'That at what time ye hear the sound of the cornet, flute, harp, sackbut, psaltery, dulcimer, and all kinds of musick, ye fall down and worship the golden image that Nebuchadnezzar the king hath set up: And whoso falleth not down and worshippeth shall the same hour be cast into the midst of a burning fiery furnace. Therefore at that time, when all the people heard the sound of the cornet, flute, harp, sackbut, psaltery, and all kinds of musick, all the people, the nations, and the languages, fell down and worshiped the golden image that Nebuchadnezzar the king had set up'?* Daniel lets us know that Nebuchadnezzar used music as the catalyst to come and worship the image of himself that he had set up.

"If that isn't a giveaway about how powerful music is, then I guess they will never get it.

"Satan is trying to control people. If those people on earth could just figure out this one thing, they would be way ahead in the race of life. The thousands of hours of music that are pumped into the heads of teenagers and adults literally swamp all of their time spent in classrooms or while reading books. Someone is going to win the battle for their minds and souls, but the only question is who?

"Someone once said, 'You let me write the songs that a nation sings, and I don't care who makes its laws.' That fatalistic music and that sexual music takes its toll on people. Suicides and the rampant sexual culture down there are coming from somewhere. I wonder why those people can't figure that out.

"Y'all remember when Paul wrote: *'Casting down imaginations, and every high thing that exalteth itself against the knowledge of God, and bringing into captivity every thought to the obedience of Christ.'* That should be a warning to everyone.

"The rock music of the world is of the world, and we don't even have to mention lyrics here. So many of the modern worship songs down there don't even mention Jesus, the cross, the blood, or so many other biblical concepts. It's almost like those people could sing the same song to their boyfriends or girlfriends, and they wouldn't even have to change one word! That is one way we know those songs don't glorify the Lord.

"One rock musician said, 'Everyone takes it for granted that rock and roll is synonymous with sex.'

"Another rock musician has said that rock music is 'the strongest drug in the world.' If that statement doesn't get someone's attention, I don't know what will.

"Rock music has always been the music of rebels and has always been sexual in nature. It has always been used as a drug. The backbeat, rhythm, and heavy syncopation create an emotional high in people.

"Studies have shown that the *high* people experience at sporting events and concerts is the same euphoric high they get at megachurches that use the same musical elements.

"And now, that same music seems to have infiltrated so many of their churches. The modern music, dancing, lights, colors, fog machines, videos, and charismatic leaders touch all of their senses and feed their flesh. The goal of church is not to entertain people but to feed truth to believers. Once you know your goal, then it is much easier to accomplish it.

"But music is one of the real keys here. Music is composed of melody, harmony, and rhythm. Melody is the most important part to music, but a rock beat literally usurps that. It then becomes the most important component of the music. The rock beat is very sensual. It is very fleshly. Repeating that sound over and over again can literally put people into an altered state of consciousness. And when that happens, anything goes. That is typically when Satan makes his move. Those people should never want to have their minds go into an altered state of consciousness whether from a drink, a drug, or the sound of certain kinds of music.

"God has cautioned those people to watch out for the lust of the flesh, the lust of the eyes, and the pride of life. He knows the things of the world can move in and keep them from living a holy life. He is warning them because He is all-knowing and they are not.

"So when we look at the world that uses rock, rap, reggae, dance, and blues music to create a worldly state of mind in people—where they drink and use drugs and dance the night away—why would Christians want to use those same rhythms and beats to try and worship the Lord? And by the way, where do we see rock concerts in the Bible?

"I am beginning to wonder how much those people down there study. All they have to know is that a backbeat puts music into a very dangerous category. That backbeat is very sensual. Secular artists have used it and continue to use it because it makes them really *feel* the music. It has been used to drive their fans wild for many years.

"It really is easy to figure out what Christian music is: It should sound different than the world! Really, that simple. If they are trying to sound like the world to reach the world, it will never work. Holy and sacred is what God is looking for. How do we know that to be true? Because that is who He is!!

"The other thing that is so easy to see is that Contemporary Christian Music (CCM) is being used in an ecumenical way to bridge the divide between people of different beliefs. That is not good. Truth is the most important thing. Doctrine matters. But music is causing people to drop their guards, which is when the false teachings seep into them. They need to have their guards up—and their guards up very high—before the Lord returns.

"The pastor of a gigantic church in Australia has said that 'we are scratching people where they are itching.' Does he realize what he is saying? Does that man read and study his Bible?

"It is written: *'For the time will come when they will not endure sound doctrine; but after their own lusts shall they heap to themselves teachers, having itching ears; And they shall turn away their ears from the truth, and shall be turned unto fables.'* That pastor is fulfilling end-time prophecy! His church is giving its people all kinds of worldly music from pop-rock and dance to EDM music, and they call it worship. They are not supposed to be giving people what they want. They are supposed to be giving them truth spoken in love! That is what people need. If they need a good dose of rock and roll, then let them go to the club, the saloon, or watch the Super Bowl Halftime Show to get it. They don't need to be feeding their flesh at church.

"Music, of course, couldn't be neutral. All they have to do is take a group of people and put a rock band in front of them. Then take the rock band away and put a symphony orchestra in its place. The people would act totally different! Also, watch how Hollywood uses music in movies. They use a certain kind of music to make people feel scared and another kind of music to make them cry. They are literally manipulating people's emotions just with the sound of the music. And if manipulation is going on, we always know who the culprit is behind that.

"Christians never want to be like the world to reach the world. They are supposed to separate from the world. If they want to be like the world, there was no need to get saved. They could have just remained in their fallen state. If they want to be just like Jesus, they will be both loved and hated; but reaching people with truth is the only option.

"It is also obvious that Satan is using this music to advance the ecumenical march away from the cross. This fleshly music will bind people of entirely different belief systems together. It will garner a tight hold on them. Satan's claws will dig deep into their flesh. They would rather stand up for their music than for the pure, unadulterated Word of God.

"Sadly, it looks like the world has become the salt in the church instead of the church and its followers being the salt of the earth. And some of those worldly songs were inspired by another spirit altogether.

"One of the rock stars they call the King of Pop once said, 'I wake up from dreams and go "Wow, put this down on paper." The whole thing is strange. You hear the words, everything is right there in front of your face. I feel that somewhere, someplace it's been done, and I'm just a courier bringing it into the world.'

"Paul McCartney of the Beatles, also known as the Fab Four, said in an interview on Larry King Live, 'The music to "Yesterday" came in a dream. The tune just came complete. You have to believe in magic. I can't read or write music.'

"Another of the Fab Four, John Lennon, said, 'It's like being possessed: like a psychic or a medium.' He also said, 'I felt like a hollow temple filled with many spirits, each one passing through me, each inhabiting me for a little time and then leaving to be replaced by another.'

"And still another singer they call The Boss went on national television to say, 'In the end you have to look at a song and not know exactly where it came from.'

"Probably the most spellbinding of them all was Led Zepplin, whose main members Robert Plant and Jimmy Page claim they don't know who wrote their occultic song 'Stairway to Heaven.' Plant has testified, 'Pagey had written the chords and played them for me. I was holding the paper and pencil, and for some reason, I was in a very bad mood. Then all of a sudden my hand was writing out words . . . I just sat there and looked at the words and then I almost leaped out of my seat.'

"So the music that brings out the beast, instead of the best, is on the rise. We can see it all over the world now. It has broken down barriers that should have never been breached. There can't be much time left. The Lord's goodness is leading people to repentance. What a merciful God that He is!!

"We can see that many of the lyrics in CCM are not very doctrinally strong, and many times, not very clear in what they are really trying to say. That is very dangerous. That is why CCM is used in the ecumenical movement. One song fits all. Sadly, if it was doctrinally strong and clear, many people probably wouldn't buy it. So I am wondering if it has more to do with selling a CD than glorifying the Lord.

"Do you remember when God wrote: *'The LORD is my strength and my shield; my heart trusted in him, and I am helped: therefore my heart greatly rejoiceth; and with my song will I praise him'?* Music is meant to praise Him. I mean *PRAISE HIM!* Believers will be doing that for all of eternity. That worship will be so beautiful! Music is not for evangelism, positivity, or to speak about contemporary issues. The Bible gives the answer. It has always been in there. Music is to be used to praise Him. Very simple.

"Another very simple giveaway is seen by going to a secular rock concert and a Christian rock concert. The fans act the same way. They make the same motions and movements with their bodies. Their arms wave and move in the same ways. That shows us, right there, the power of the music that is being played. It produces the same response in both Christians and non-Christians alike.

"We can also see that some of the Christian singers and bands are turning into idols. They sell t-shirts, hats, wristbands, and all the other paraphernalia, just like secular bands do. They do autograph signings, just like the secular bands do. How does that glorify the Lord? It sure looks like it glorifies them and not the Lord.

"One big traveling Christian concert has video games, high-wire acts, skateboarding, BMX bikes, and all of these other worldly things for the kids to do before the worldly music starts. How is that drawing the students closer to Jesus? They need to be reading the Bible. They need to be studying the Word of God. They need to be trained up in soul winning and tear that city up for the Lord! But what is the problem? That won't draw five or ten thousand people. They probably won't sell many tickets for that. They probably won't make much money on that type of event.

"Why do they want to use the ways of the world to reach the lost? The music and movies they are trying to use don't glorify Him. If Jesus wanted to use all of that because it was the best way to reach folks, then He would have used those means when He was there. Why can't they just see that talking to people and giving people literature is the best route to reach the lost? That is exactly how they did it in biblical times.

"Trying to be like the world to reach the world has never worked in all of history, and it won't work in the final days before His return.

"One group that is trying to do this is the Emerging Church movement. Thinking that a church would ever have to adapt to the culture around it is ludicrous. It is Christians who should be changing the culture with truth and love and being salt and light, rather than letting the surrounding culture seep into their churches. History is littered with the trouble caused when the followers of God turn towards the world.

"We can tell that these emergent leaders who are leading people in the wrong directions are much more concerned about elevating feelings over truth. How one *feels* about something is more important than if something is actually true. Just because someone feels like God would not create a hell doesn't mean He didn't make one! These are dangerous teachings.

"Truth becomes relative to this group. Truth is not absolute. So it keeps changing with the times. If that were a true statement, then they could never plant their feet firmly on the Word of God and not budge. But that is what they are supposed to be doing! Saying that truth is relative is a direct attack on God's holy words.

"This movement wants their experiences to top reason. They want to follow the music, the icons, the images, the candles, and the incense more than just sitting down and digging through the Word of God to find its beautiful, eternal truths to apply to their lives.

"This type of thinking always leads to a more liberal view of theology and Scripture. Many times, the emergent church gets intertwined with the *social gospel*. Basically, the social gospel is about meeting people's physical needs. So in their own towns or even when going on mission trips, they build water wells, try to eradicate hunger, perform dental and medical procedures, rescue people from slavery and prostitution, help the homeless, and sometimes help them out financially. But for many, that is all they are doing! Many of their mission trips don't ever include sharing Jesus with the lost people there. Or, they downplay repentance, the cross, and the blood. We never see anything like that in the Bible.

"They should realize that a lot of those trips just make their flesh feel good. They feel good about having accomplished something. But every one of the souls they help is going to die. Every one of them will take their last breath. Every one of them will be crossing over to the other side. And every one of them needs Jesus to make sure they have a successful, eternal journey.

"Jesus commands them to go into all the world and preach the gospel to every creature; and sadly, many of them just want to go and give them a cup of water. What they really need is living water, just like the woman at the well. She is eternally grateful that Jesus gave her what she truly needed.

"Also in the emergent movement, it seems they are okay in uniting with each other over error, rather than dividing from error to uphold truth. If they could see it from our perspective, they sure would see it differently. We know for sure that truth always trumps unity.

"You just begin to wonder why doesn't the church of the end times look like the church in the book of Acts.

"And one of the great errors roaming the earth these days is called Replacement theology. Its basic premise is that God's plan for Israel is now over with. They are no longer the chosen people. When they rejected Messiah, they were then cast aside; and now, all of the promises for Israel have been given to the Church.

"We would think they could figure out by looking at a map of the Middle East that God is not done with Israel yet! It has been fascinating to watch Him bring the Jews back to their homeland. What a sight to behold and what a journey for so many of them.

"The Church and Israel are completely distinct in Scripture. God has different functions and different roles for them, just like He has different roles for men and women. Clearly, the literal interpretation of Scripture shows that God is not done yet with Israel. When people allegorize God's words, they get into trouble.

"Also, this teaching can lead to anti-Semitism. We have seen throughout history the danger of that mindset and where it leads. God has not cast off His chosen people. God has not cast off Israel. God wants them to repent and be saved, and every true believer should want the same.

"One thing people can never forget is that everyone has a *yarmulke* in this fight. If they let the Jews be run over, it should not surprise them when they are run over next. But if the promises of God to the Jews can be allegorized, then it's not surprising if other biblical truths can be allegorized, too.

"Another real and obvious danger they face is the blending of different religions together. We see that occurring in many of these movements, but it is also happening in something they are calling *Chrislam:* the mixing together of Christianity with the religion of Islam.

"Now that is a new one to us! Why would that even cross someone's mind down there? The only way it can cross their mind is if they decide to not take seriously the cross of Jesus Christ. Since Islam teaches that Jesus did not even die on the cross, and that He did not rise from the dead three days later, those two religions are as far apart as the earth and the sun.

"Such thinking will lead to the many paths to Heaven argument. That they can take any path they want to be right with God: the Muslim path, the Hindu path, the Buddhist path, or the good works path, and we will all end up at the same destination.

"Those folks need to wake up quickly because there are two destinations on this side—not one—and only one path to get to the right one.

"Jesus is God. But Islam says in the Qur'an that it is blasphemous to say that Jesus is God, and it teaches Allah had no son. Remember, truth will always come down to the deity of Jesus Christ. Once people figure out who Jesus is, the rest is easy.

"People down there need to wise up quickly because those two religions do not worship the same God. We know that for sure!

"But because the Qur'an mentions Jesus 25 times, some people think that Christianity and Islam can be syncretized together.

"The other thing we can tell is that people want peace. They want peace in the Middle East. So if they can have peace between these two major religions, then there will be peace surrounding them. The only problem, of course, is that they cannot have true peace without the Prince of Peace! Everything else is a counterfeit of the real thing.

"And sadly, as the finish line approaches, Satan is once again playing with God's words. It is a dastardly trick. He has trapped many souls that way, but it's like he has really stepped up his game.

"If he cannot stop people from reading the Bible—which he has done to so many people walking the streets of Earth—then he will try and get them a Bible that is messed up. That has false things in it. That way, they cannot tell what the truth is and what the lie is. He will deceive them any which way that he can. The closer he can move the lie next to the truth, the harder it will be to detect.

"In many of the English Bibles that have flooded the market in the last century, there have been subtle changes and outright blasphemy in them. But since they say *Bible* on the front of the book, people put their guards down. And when their guards are down, the enemy always stands a great chance for success.

"Changing things like referring to Jesus as *He* rather than as *God*. Shortening His title of Lord Jesus Christ to separate His deity from His humanity. Failing to credit Him as the Creator in some passages. Omitting references to Him being worshiped as God. Neglecting to recognize His eternal nature in places. There are changes that question the virgin birth. And some newer versions even attribute Jesus' title of Morning Star to Lucifer, who is actually the son of the morning. So when those changes take place, it is always an attack on the deity of Jesus Christ. And we know, Satan has always tried to attack the real identity of Jesus.

"The word *blood* is removed numerous times in some of the newer translations. It is only the blood of Jesus that can cleanse people of their sins. 'Nothing but the blood' of Jesus, yet that blood is literally taken out of certain scriptures in those Bibles. Satan knows people need a perfect blood sacrifice when they meet God, and he is trying to do everything he can to keep them from realizing that.

"The removal of the word *hell* from some Bible versions is just stunning. Satan is trying to deceive people into thinking there won't be a hell for the unbeliever. Don't worry about it. That place doesn't exist. That is why God repeats it over fifty times in the Bible. He doesn't want anyone to miss the point. If you are not born again, Hell is your eternal destination.

"The Holy Spirit-inspired Bible says: *'. . . for thou hast magnified thy word above all thy name.'* God also said, *'For ever, O LORD, thy word is settled in heaven.'* God isn't playing around here. Satan is playing around; and some people on earth are playing around for a profit, but God means business. His Word matters. He doesn't waste words. It is settled. This book has been branded, just like a good horse. You know who the owner is, and there will never be any mistaking who is the true Author of the Bible! And, of course, that book is branded in the blood of Christ, and many people have spilled their blood to protect the words of that book through the centuries.

"Jesus also stated: *'Heaven and earth shall pass away, but my words shall not pass away.'* God's true words aren't going anywhere no matter what type of fight or deception Satan puts up. John penned: *'Sanctify them through thy truth: thy word is truth.'* Satan lies and people die. God knows that His Word brings truth and life to people both on earth and for eternity.

"God meant business when He had Moses write: *'Ye shall not add unto the word which I command you, neither shall ye diminish ought from it.'* Adding to or taking away from God's words is going to bring the hand of God against many. They need to take His Book much more seriously than they currently do.

"Just to add emphasis, God said, *'Add thou not unto his words, lest he reprove thee, and thou be found a liar.'* All liars will inherit a lake of fire, so that should be a strong enough warning for those humans to not mess around with what God has said.

"And if anyone is not clear about how important God's Word is and how He will uphold and preserve it, or how seriously people on earth need to take it, He said, *'The words of the LORD are pure words: as silver tried in a furnace of earth, purified seven times. Thou shalt keep them, O LORD, thou shalt preserve them from this generation for ever.'*

"This just shows how Satan is on the prowl. We know he has a job to do. We know he is good at his job. If people would read and study their Bibles, and even just look at the names for Satan, they would find out so much more about his character and what he is trying to accomplish. His names are Abaddon, accuser of our brethren, adversary, angel of the bottomless pit, Apollyon, Beelzebub, Belial, crooked serpent, dragon, enemy, evil spirit, father of lies, great red dragon, leviathan, liar, lying spirit, murderer, old serpent, piercing serpent, power of darkness, prince of this world, prince of the devils, prince of the power of the air, ruler of the darkness of this world, Satan, serpent, spirit that worketh in the children of disobedience, tempter, the god of this world, unclean spirit, and the wicked one. So what do you guys think of those names?!" Elap proclaimed.

"Wow," Onyx retorted. "What a list! You really see his whole character just by looking at his names. They show what he is all about and what he is up to. This isn't someone you would invite to a Polo match. You wouldn't want him to mount you and take you for a ride. Matter of fact, you don't want him anywhere near you or your friends. Yet, we watch from a distance. We see people all the time just play with Satan. They let him in their lives. They open up the door to him. They treat him like a toy. Like he is harmless, yet he is going in for the kill. He plays for keeps, and those people just play. He wants their hearts. He is so good at what he does that many people don't even know they are under his sway. They don't know they have taken a bite from the wrong piece of fruit. What a master of his craft he really is.

"His hatred for God is paramount. He can't unseat the King. No one can. So what is the next best thing in his stable of tricks? Get people to not become born again or get believers to not live out the plan God has for them. The adversary of God doesn't rest. He is busy. He is on the hunt. He is looking for those whom he can devour. Serious business here. No games for him. His last chance to get at the King before his eternal consignment to a lake of fire. This is literally a death match between these two. Satan knows he will be an eternal loser, but he is not going down without a fight.

"Genesis lets us know that men and women are made in the image of God, and they are now Satan's prey. He has a laser-like focus to destroy lives. People think they are playing with a kitty cat instead of with a roaring lion. They better repent and stop giving him a foothold in their lives. They better wake up before it is way too late for them.

"The stakes are so high that God uses some strong words to get people's attention. He is that serious. We can tell that no one down there wants to be called a *whore*. That word has such a bad connotation. It is used in different ways, but none of them is positive. If someone ever says that of another person, it is always meant in a negative light; and no one likes it."

"I know where you are going with this," Elap elaborated.

"Yup. Ninety times in the Bible, God uses that exact same term! Yes, it is used to refer to sleeping around with people they shouldn't, but its main use is very, very different. It's a term used to describe people who chase different gods. They go *a-whoring* after those other gods. They are prostituting themselves with those other gods. Those gods cannot satisfy. They give a temporary pleasure. Nothing more. The lust of the eyes, the lust of the flesh, and the pride of life can bring them temporary pleasure, but those sins will bite in the end and bring them eternal destruction.

"God has given all of these people His truth. He parted the Red Sea for them. He brought them manna from Heaven.

He protected them when the trials and tribulations came. He gave them His Son. He has given them a peace that passes all understanding. Yet, they are not satisfied. Yet, it is time to chase something else: the god of money; the god of pleasure; the god of sports; the god of fame; the god of alcohol and drugs; the god of visual entertainment; and the gods of different religions that can't do anything for them now or for eternity. They are whoring around. They are prostituting themselves when God has given them the real thing. They are the bride of Christ, but they would rather cheat on their Husband. They say you are good for tonight, but I have other desires. They have a faithful Partner, but their eyes are wandering. They see something that looks better at the moment, and they start the slow process of walking away and cheating on their Mate. That is why He refers to them as *whoring* around. That is a serious term. Nobody down there would want the word *WHORE* stamped on their forehead. They would wear a stocking cap pulled down to their eyes every day, no matter how hot it was. But that is what they are. That is what they are doing.

"Time and time again, Scriptures talk about the people of God provoking His anger against them. They are poking their finger in His eye. They go a-whoring around after other gods. He has done so much for them, but they go wandering after other things and act like He doesn't even exist. I have no clue why they would want to stir God up. He only wants the best for them. He has shown that is what He wants for them over and over. Yet, it is almost like they don't care. Some of them better wake up because He cares about them big time!

"That is why God said, *'Or despisest thou the riches of his goodness and forbearance and longsuffering; not knowing that the goodness of God leadeth thee to repentance?'* He is so kind. He is so gracious. He is slow to anger; and it looks like people are taking advantage of that, and they shouldn't. He wants the people who are living in sin and whoring around after other gods to repent and come back to His loving arms and embrace. He loves them so dearly. He is the groom who would never leave them nor ever forsake them. What a heart He has! What compassion! We know that, but they need to know that, before it is too late. Time is running short. The race is coming to a close. The finish line is just ahead. Whores don't win in the end. Forgiven whores and repentant whores will have a joyous eternity with their Companion!!

"Do you remember when God wrote: *'In those days there was no king in Israel: every man did that which was right in his own eyes'*? If Jesus is not their King, it looks like they will literally do anything that their eyes lead them to do. It has become that bad.

"What really is going on with all of these movements is that the judgment of God is coming upon the church. God has warned against all of these things from His Word. It is the only Source of Truth, it has stood the test of time throughout the millennia, and it tells people right from wrong. Tells them what is of God and what is not of God. But when people arrogantly put their thoughts, ideas, and practices above the Word of God, they are essentially saying that they are God. They know what is best. The truth of the matter is Father knows best. He has always known what is best. He wouldn't leave His people without truth. That would be so unkind, and there is not an unkind part in His entire Being. He is 100% love and truth all throughout Him.

"God wrote through Jude to the dwellers of earth: *'Beloved, when I gave all diligence to write unto you of the common salvation, it was needful for me to write unto you, and exhort you that ye should earnestly contend for the faith which was once delivered unto the saints.'* People need to fight. They need to fight for the faith. They are contenders in a prize fight and not spectators in the arena.

"Paul let everyone know, *'And have no fellowship with the unfruitful works of darkness, but rather reprove them.'* Darkness is ugly. Darkness is not of God. People should be exposing it and not running to it. But if they are afraid of what people think of them, afraid of losing friends, afraid of not having a big ministry, or afraid of losing money, they will keep their mouths shut and let people around them be deceived.

"Paul also said, *'Prove all things; hold fast that which is good.'* Test. Test. Test. Pretty simple. Test and verify. Testing everything will protect their hearts, their family's hearts, and their church's hearts.

"Paul wasn't done. He is serious about this. He wrote: *'Now I beseech you, brethren, mark them which cause divisions and offences contrary to the doctrine which ye have learned; and avoid them.'* Correct doctrine is so, so important to God. Truth is truth. Satan will always try to muddy the waters. It is easy to figure out when he is at work because what he does will never align with God's Word.

"Watch what Matthew said about this when he wrote: *'Then Jesus said unto them, Take heed and beware of the leaven of the Pharisees and of the Sadducees. And they reasoned among themselves, saying, It is because we have taken no bread. Which when Jesus perceived, he said unto them, O ye of little faith, why reason ye among yourselves, because ye have brought no bread? Do ye not yet understand, neither remember the five loaves of the five thousand, and how many baskets ye took up? Neither the seven loaves of the four thousand, and how many baskets ye took up? How is it that ye do not understand that I spake it not to you concerning bread, that ye should beware of the leaven of the Pharisees and of the Sadducees?'* Leaven spreads and infests the whole loaf. That is exactly what false teaching does, as well.

"They need to avoid those with these false doctrines. Call them out, so others will not be ensnared by their false ways. It is much easier to prevent people from getting into false teachings than it is to rescue them once they have succumbed to the enemy.

"This is really not that difficult to figure out. Satan always tries to lay traps. He puts snares out there and tries to catch people. It is like walking down a pathway, and part of it is covered with leaves. What the people don't know is there is a deep, dark chasm beneath those leaves, but they keep walking. They keep going forward. There are signs all around warning them not to go in that direction. To stop. Do a U-turn. Danger ahead. But it is like they either don't care or they have let Satan deceive them to the point they don't realize the serious danger that is lurking ahead.

"Those folks down there seem to want to be friends with everyone. That is not what the Scriptures call for. They need to be friends with truth. They need to be friends with Jesus. All the rest of it will work itself out down there or up here."

"How many times did Jesus tell people to *'follow Me'*?" Onyx asked.

"I am not sure I can count that high! It was a huge part of His ministry and a huge part of His teaching to His followers. Remember when He said to His disciples, *'If any man will come after me, let him deny himself, and take up his cross, and follow me'?* This is serious business to Him," Elap noted.

"Follow Him, follow Him, follow Him would probably be the best guidance anyone could have after being saved. It simplifies everything. Read His Word, and obey His Word. Follow His teachings. Do what He did. Behave like He did. Jesus didn't worry about what others said about Him. He wasn't overly concerned with their opinions of Him. He knew He was God incarnate and His death and resurrection would prove it. He was determined to do what was right. All done in love. That is His character.

"Those people need to do the same, before it is too late. When they get off track, anything is possible. It would be like them running their horseless carriages into ditch after ditch and then keep doing the same thing again and again. They name their horseless carriages after us and call them Pintos, Broncos, and Mustangs; but we would never gallop off into a ditch. And then they tell us how much horsepower one of those horseless carriages has!

"People sure are funny, but what they need to do is stand up for what is right. Stand up for truth. Stand up in love, and let the chips fall where they may. They need to never forget that He owns all of the chips. It doesn't matter if they fall over sometimes.

He can stack them back up the way He wants to at any time. They just need to grab the reins, follow Him, and never look back!

"They need to ask themselves: If they were crossing the Red Sea at the time of Moses, would they have been dry or would they have been wet? A lot of people and a lot of horses died that day. None of the Egyptians would obey God and be faithful to Him. God makes it so easy, and people seem to make it so hard.

"Will they board the Ark of Safety that God provides? Only one door and one way to get on board, and it is through the blood of Jesus Christ. If not, then they are going to get wet as God brings His flood of judgment on those who hate Him.

"It was once said that a soldier fights because he hates what is in front of him and loves what is behind him. Those Christians down there need to love the Lord who is front of them and the people who are behind them! That will keep them dry until they meet the One who gave them living water!

"When His Word said: *'Let us hear the conclusion of the whole matter: Fear God, and keep his commandments: for this is the whole duty of man. For God shall bring every work into judgment, with every secret thing, whether it be good, or whether it be evil,'* He meant it. Finish well!

"Did you see what that teenager just wrote, Onyx?"

Let me tell you a bit about my journey, so far, as an evangelizer . . . I'm 16 and doubted by the world (because she's 16 what could she possibly know, right?), I'm often rejected (because who wants to be proven wrong by a little kid, right?), I'm considered annoying (because who wants some "punk" trying to talk to them, right?), I'm looked down upon (because they have been on this earth longer, right?), I'm ignored (because that kid couldn't possibly have anything worth their time, right?), I'm pushed away (because who has time to hear a child ramble on, right?), I'm turned down (because who wants to look weak in the eyes of a kid, right?), I'm yelled at (because who wants to be told they're going to Hell, right?), I'm laughed at (because who wants to hear that everything they've ever been taught is false, right?), and I'm quizzed (because who doesn't want to watch a kid squirm, right?). I have days that I just cry because I know people are entering Hell as I sit in my cozy bed, ready for eternity and with no fear of death. I get depressed sometimes, because someone I know dies without knowing the love Jesus offers. I get angry, because I wish I was bolder to share the gospel. I get frustrated, because I should've said something else over what I ended up saying. I get confused because sometimes God's will isn't mine (praise Him for that, though). I get sad, because the world lacks passion. I get annoyed, because no one seems to care that people are going to Hell. I get scared, because what if I say the wrong thing? I get nervous, because I put the pressure on myself, forgetting God's in control and will give me the right words to speak. I get doubtful, cause what are the odds that I actually have the truth? I have flaws, I have failures, but you know what? I also serve a perfect God who doesn't have ANY of that. And there will be days I'm lacking faith in God, but that's not going to stop me from sharing my faith.

I WILL tell the world. I WILL obey my God. I WILL run to my God, and I WILL run hard. I WILL spread the love of God. I WILL not stop until every knee bows at the throne of God.

I WILL NOT give up.

"Oh my, Satan is going to have trouble with that one! She is one that will not bow her knee to him. God gave her life, and she is giving her life back to Him! Way to go!!

"The writings of the Apostle John are so appropriate at this time: *'Verily, verily, I say unto you, Except a corn of wheat fall into the ground and die, it abideth alone: but if it die, it bringeth forth much fruit. He that loveth his life shall lose it; and he that hateth his life in this world shall keep it unto life eternal. If any man serve me, let him follow me; and where I am, there shall also my servant be: if any man serve me, him will my Father honour.'*

"She is dead to the things of the world and now will be used mightily by the Lord. Jesus takes no pleasure in the death of the wicked, and neither does she! She is just like those biblical watchmen we have seen throughout the centuries. I wonder if more are going to sign up to be watchmen, before it is too late.

"We definitely want to think about the seriousness of reducing truth to mere opinion or dismissing it as a side issue. Truth matters. It is anything but a peripheral issue. Pilate said, *'What is truth?'* Jesus rebuked the Pharisees over truth. The Pharisees put Jesus to death because of truth. The apostles warned the church to watch out for deceivers who didn't teach truth. Jesus is Truth incarnate. Truth is everything. Without it, we have nothing but shifting sands. In fact, to dismiss truth as peripheral is dangerous territory.

"All of time is dated from the embryo in Mary's womb. If that doesn't tell people that Jesus is Someone they should be putting their eyes upon, I don't know what will get their attention.

"The hour is late. They have the last piece of truth they will ever need: The Holy Bible! The clock is ticking down. We are about to go. The starter pistol is about to be shot. Are those people ready for a Stakes Race that has eternal consequences?"

The four of them fell silent as they looked off in the distance. The end was in sight. Onyx broke the silence by saying, "Well, guys, it looks like these are our last steps. The end of the road is right up ahead. The trotting is done. We're about to gallop at full speed. We're down to the wire now."

"Didn't God always give His best to mankind? And didn't we see His truth being ignored and replaced over and over again? What more could He have done? Corruption seeped into everything, even into the very things that were dedicated to Him," Elap said with regret.

Chapter 22
The Last Bastion of Hope

"**Jesus is Lord of Heaven** and Earth, and He walks amongst the churches. But someone else is prowling around the churches, too. Jesus knows that Satan is going to play his hand of self-deception. He's going to try and get people to merely talk about truth instead of being involved in living that truth. Satan knows if they live out that truth, he'll be defeated before he even gets out of the gate," Crimson expounded.

"The Church at Ephesus was pastored by the Apostle John. Many people think of him as the Apostle of Love, and he was; yet, the Ephesian church had lost their first love. All roads converged in Ephesus. The Temple of Diana was also there, which was one of the Seven Wonders of the Ancient World.

"Ephesus was a backslidden church. They had lost the vitality of the Christian life. They were working hard, standing for truth, identifying false doctrine and false teachers, and were busy with the things of the Lord, but they weren't in love with the Lord. Perhaps their work had pulled them away, and it is possible they mistook their strong stand and discernment as loving the Lord when what He wanted was their hearts.

"Too many times Christians are living half a Christian life. They have the armchair quarterback thing going on, but they aren't actually living out the Christian life. They keep busy with things of the church, but not with the things of the Lord. They stay busy with programs, activities, studies, families, and discernment instead of the deeds they did at first.

"What do most people do when they first become born again? They share their faith with others constantly. They want to please the Lord at all costs and love others unconditionally. They willingly sacrifice for the Lord. They are excited to give and excited about the things of God. They talk about Him continually. He is their first love. People need to get back to those days. That is when they will truly have the most joy in their lives. We can see it in their countenances, and what a sight it is to behold!

"The Church of Smyrna was a persecuted and suffering church. Smyrna was a beautiful city, and its name comes from the burial spice myrrh. It was a well-planned and well-organized city, and it literally had a street of gold with Zeus at the west end and Diana at the east end. The Christians there were willing to go to their death rather than honor Caesar.

"Persecution is the full-on attack from Satan. He will use brute force, imprisonment, torture, and imminent death to try and wipe out true believers and the church. Satan will always try to get Christians to bow to idolatry at the threat of death. 'Bow or else' is his mantra. Compromise is not of the Lord. What will people do when this moment arises in their lives?

"Followers of the Lord will always have to make choices. Christians in Smyrna were losing everything to stand firm for Christ. In the world's eyes, they had nothing; but Jesus said they had it all. They were rich because they had Him! Will they compromise, or will they stand strong?

"If this means becoming a living sacrifice as the real fragrant offering of devotion to Christ in their death, so be it. They would rather die than betray Christ with even the slightest hint of compromise. What a beautiful relationship they have with the Lord!

"All they have to know are the words of Jesus to realize how seriously He takes all of this. He has told them, *'Whosoever therefore shall confess me before men, him will I confess also before my Father which is in heaven. But whosoever shall deny me before men, him will I also deny before my Father which is in heaven. Think not that I am come to send peace on earth: I came not to send*

*peace, but a sword. For I am come to set a man at variance against
his father, and the daughter against her mother, and the daughter
in law against her mother in law. And a man's foes shall be they
of his own household. He that loveth father or mother more than
me is not worthy of me: and he that loveth son or daughter more
than me is not worthy of me. And he that taketh not his cross, and
followeth after me, is not worthy of me. He that findeth his life
shall lose it: and he that loseth his life for my sake shall find it.'*
Time for people to lose their lives in the Lord Jesus Christ.

"I wonder if Christians today give that any thought at all.
Compromise is everywhere as we view earth. Some who call
themselves *Christian* can cave quickly to pressure and compromise. What if they had the faith of these Smyrna believers? Their
strong stand would spread the gospel. It would literally explode
the gospel across the world like a nuclear weapon. But we can
tell Satan has many people more worried about their present
circumstances than about what is best for the gospel and the
kingdom of God.

"And Jesus will give them the crown of life to boot! No
believer has to ever worry about the second death. His followers
just need to be faithful. He will take care of the rest.

"Sadly, the Church at Pergamos was a compromising church.
Pergamos means 'mixed marriage,' and this happens to mean
the marriage between the church and the world system. The city
was a center for pagan idolatry. It was the capital of the Roman
province of Asia and the seat of pagan authority. Its immense
altar to Zeus was the largest altar in the ancient world. Sadly,
even Christians celebrated pagan rituals and feast days when
they should not have.

"Interestingly, the church at Ephesus kept the deeds of the
Nicolaitans out, but the church at Pergamos let their doctrine
in. The deeds of the Nicolaitans were tolerated and no longer
rejected like they were in Ephesus. This is a sign of compromise,
and that never, ever ends well.

"Jesus identifies Himself as the one with the two-edged sword. We know what that means. The Word is able to cut through their agenda and cut them to the quick. The Word judges them now and will judge them in the end. If they will repent and follow His Word, they will be fine. If not, trouble is galloping towards them.

"Satan is always in attack mode. Satan tries to water down Christianity by making it acceptable in the eyes of the world, which opens the door for Christians to become worldly. That compromise pollutes the church, pollutes the truth, pollutes the gospel, and always brings judgment.

"He also entices them with the promise of power, which so many believers really want. They make the fatal error, many times, of marrying the church to political power. Power comes and power goes on planet Earth. We have seen kingdoms come and kingdoms go all through history. The worldly power system just uses Christians for their votes and their money. Sadly, many of them don't see it until they are entrapped and entangled by the enemy. By then it is typically, in their minds, too late to escape his web. The key is to get out of his web immediately, before it is too late.

"Jesus always sets the highest standard. He has wed Himself to the church, not to the world. Why? He is not of this world and doesn't want His bride to be of the world either. When the church keeps the pollution of the world far away, she remains unspotted and loyal to Him.

"Remember when Satan promised Jesus the kingdoms of the world, but Jesus refused? The church should refuse, too. Now that might not sound like a good earthly choice, but that is an excellent eternal choice!

"We can still see churches uniting with governments today. The government puts restrictions on what they can and can't say. That compromise will never lead to the destruction of government but only to the destruction of the visible church. Truth can never take a backseat. Truth cannot be compromised. Either truth is in the front seat, or it is nowhere to be found.

"Jesus always takes care of His people! He gives them hidden manna and a pure white stone, which represent what is clean and pure to the overcomers who follow Him. His love and care for His people and His church are literally out of that world! They need to be overcomers until they see Him face to face!!

"The Church of Thyatira was a very important church; yet at the same time, it became very lax. *Thyatira* means 'continual sacrifice.' That is a good lesson for all. They must continually be in the Word of God, continually seeking God, continually praying, continually being a servant, or they will leave an opening for the enemy to come in. He will see that breach and make his move, and it literally can be deadly.

"Thyatira wasn't on a major trade route, but it was a military garrison located on a plain, so it tended to be invaded a lot. *No protection* typically means more invasions. So simple, but I wish those humans would understand that.

"This city was known for its commerce and powerful trade guilds. These guilds were like unions, and each one of them worshiped their own deity. So what did that mean for believers? They were put in the position of having to compromise what they believed to work in one of those guilds.

"God does that so often. He is always testing those He loves. He is putting them through the furnace of His love. Will they choose a job or Him? Will they choose popularity or Him? Those choices are endless, but there is only One right answer to every one of those tests that He puts in front of them.

"God is not happy with the woman Jezebel who is influencing those people. She is teaching and seducing them, and it looks like they don't even recognize it. She has lulled them to sleep with her false teachings, and that is one of the most dangerous positions any believer can ever find themselves in. Her teachings shouldn't have been allowed because they were deadly. Why don't those people rebuke and shun this false prophetess?

"Jesus, of course, is so gracious by giving Jezebel time to repent of her deeds. His kindness always shines through. But Jesus' eyes are like a flame of fire. They are a penetrating gaze into their hearts. Nothing escapes Him. He knows all. Trying to hide things from Him or pull the blinders over His eyes is literally a total waste of time. Repent and come clean. It works every time.

"Satan's attack here is so obvious. He tries to attack the church from within. He has always tried that and has had great success with this tactic throughout the centuries. He will try and get his satanic practices inside of churches; and if that doesn't work, then he will try something else like withholding employment from true believers. He will hit them in their pocketbook to see if they will still trust the King.

"The Church of Sardis was one of the most important churches in Asia Minor. The city of Sardis was built on steep rocks and was nearly impregnable. So what does that often lead to? They thought of themselves as safe and invincible. We will always be here. Nothing can stop us. Of course, God destroyed that city with an earthquake!

"That is exactly what happened to the Church of Sardis. They thought they were fine, but they were dead. That church looked alive on the outside, but it was truly dead on the inside.

"We can see that all across the world. Even some of the churches that seem to be hopping with all of the bells and whistles and have big attendance are dead on the inside. No personal passion to live for Jesus. It's like they check *going to church* off their list, have some kind of experience, and then go and enjoy an afternoon football game or a car race. Boy, have they been deceived. And sadly, many of them don't even know it.

"Persecution has been part of the lifeblood of the church for centuries. Pain and suffering have strengthened the believer and the church to stand strong. We have seen it all through Earth's history. That is not what is going on here. When the church was persecuted, it grew. When it was deceived, it fell apart. People just need to discern what is going on, and then that will lead them to the pathway they need to take.

"It is easy to see the progression of these churches and the progression of churches throughout history. In Ephesus, they had works without love. In Pergamos, it was worldly and flirting with sin. Thyatira was fully in sin; and now in Sardis, the church is dead.

"When Satan deceives, he can make it all seem so religious; but it is literally so dead. Things like *church membership saves* or *acting religious* is good enough. Large attendance and big buildings must mean vitality, when they don't. The pride of being unteachable is so dangerous because they can't fathom they're wrong. Pride ends up nullifying the truth that is convicting them. Resting on the past is a sure-fire way to get off track. Thinking that small compromises don't matter when they have always led to bigger ones down the road. Compromise always matters with the Lord.

"Apathy has overtaken this church. Not repenting is really a choice to stay asleep. When they believe teachings that can't be shouted from the rooftops, something is very, very wrong. They need to repent of their false doctrine and dead religiosity, and move on to living humbly and on fire for the Lord Jesus Christ! But there are always a faithful few. God always has a remnant!

"The city of Philadelphia was devastated by the same earthquake that hit Sardis in 17 A.D. Tremors lasted for twenty years, and people were constantly leaving their homes because of them. But being shaken up is not a bad thing. It keeps them on edge. It is good for a church, as well, so they don't get comfortable.

"The Church of Philadelphia was full of the Spirit of God. It had zeal for the Lord, was alive, and stayed on fire for the Lord for a long time!

"Missionary activity is what keeps a church on fire. Being on the front lines keeps that zeal and passion hot, hot, hot!

Missionary activity is the greatest show of brotherly love. How can people say they love someone but not tell them about Jesus and what awaits them when they die? That is anathema to God.

"But as you fellas know, when the real work of God is being done, then here comes the enemy. Satan is never far behind to try and mess things up. The synagogue of Satan is on the move. We have seen throughout history that he is always looking to counterfeit things. False religions and false teachings are his game. Anything to pull people away from biblical truth. His game is so easy to spot. I keep wondering why so many people fall for his antics?

"But, of course, Jesus trumps anything Satan can throw out there! He has set before them an open door that no man can shut. Jesus is so gracious in opening so many doors for evangelism. His people just need to walk right through them with the banner of the Lord held very high!

"The hour of temptation will come upon the whole world, but not to those who keep His Word, persevere, and uphold Jesus' Name. Jesus can come very quickly. Death can come without a moment's notice. Life goes by so very quickly. They just need to hold fast. He will rescue them in due course. And when Jesus writes a new name upon them, all of their tribulations and trials for Him will be very worth it in that day!

"You guys remember when Peter wrote: *'Knowing this first, that there shall come in the last days scoffers, walking after their own lusts, And saying, Where is the promise of his coming? for since the fathers fell asleep, all things continue as they were from the beginning of the creation. For this they willingly are ignorant of, that by the word of God the heavens were of old, and the earth standing out of the water and in the water: Whereby the world that then was, being overflowed with water, perished: But the heavens and the earth, which are now, by the same word are kept in store, reserved unto fire against the day of judgment and perdition of ungodly men.'* It is like people don't realize that the last days are all around them. But even more interesting, so many of them are the fulfillment of these Scriptures, and they can't even see it.

"The atheists and agnostics are true definitions of scoffers. Many of them mock and ridicule true believers and the Most Holy Word of God. They just can't sit back and let Christians live. They must attack. They try to seek and destroy, and that is a very bad long-term strategy.

"Throughout history, most men believed in divine creation. They knew God had to have—and did—create what was around them. Now people are derided and scorned if they do not bow at the altar of Darwinian evolution. It has been fascinating to watch this throughout the years.

"Lies always evaporate away. Truth always triumphs over untruth. Many people down there try and change the facts to fit their theories, but it is always better to stick with the facts. Truth will win out. We know that for sure.

"We can see that they have put their intellect above the Word of God, and by doing so, they have made themselves a god in their own minds. They will not humble themselves to come to the Lord. That *me-first* attitude always leads to destruction. If they would truly get back to being earnest lovers of truth, life would be so simple for them to figure out.

"Those mockers continue to deny the divine creation of planet Earth and the global flood. When it was time for judgment, God sent a worldwide flood. Now they say it was a bunch of local floods; and if anyone believes in a worldwide flood, they are considered fools. Yet, we saw Him do it! We know it was a worldwide flood. But even if they don't want to believe the Scriptures, all they have to do is look at a globe or get on a cruise ship. It's so obvious from here. Seventy percent of the earth's surface is covered in water!! Where do they think all of that water came from?! What do they think happened? Secretariat's water trough tipped over, and it covered seventy percent of the earth with water?!! Who are they trying to kid? The evidence is right before them, and they truly just do not want to believe it. Funny, though, we saw the whole thing take place! We watched Him marvelously put together this universe. And what He did with planet Earth is literally out of this world!

"Another amazing thing is how dogmatic the scientific community has become in saying the earth has to be billions of years old. Now, we know why they do that. They know they need many billions of years for macroevolution to be even remotely possible. Of course, we know it is a young earth. We have watched history unfold! We are still here watching it. What a fascinating journey it has been to see all of this play itself out. All anyone needs to do, whether scientist or average person, is look at the evidence. Just take a look at the bent rock layers; soft tissue in fossils; rapidly decaying magnetic field; carbon-14 in fossils, coal, and diamonds; and DNA found in supposedly ancient bacteria. The evidence is screaming that the earth is very young. But if they have ear plugs, ear muffs, a scarf or two wrapped around their head, and bury their head in the sand, then facts can't penetrate the false wall they have erected! Science says young earth. The Bible says young earth. It is a young earth.

"And all of this denying of God's creation and this accepting of Darwinian evolution means people have walked away from the divine inspiration of the Bible. And if God didn't create this grand universe, then there is no reason for them to waste their time trying to figure out how they got there and where they will be going when they die. Let's see what some other people had to say about this subject:

> "So irresistible are these evidences of an intelligent and powerful Agent that, of the infinite numbers of men who have exited thro' all the time, they have believed, in the proportion of a million at least to Unit, in the hypothesis of an eternal pre-existence of a creator, rather than in that of a self-existent Universe."
> **—Thomas Jefferson, Third American President**

"The more I study nature, the more I stand amazed
at the work of the Creator."
"Science brings men nearer to God."
—Louis Pasteur, French chemist and microbiologist

"Oh Lord, thou givest us everything, at the price of an effort."
—Leonardo da Vinci, Renaissance genius

"I can see how it might be possible for a man to look down upon
earth and be an atheist, but I cannot conceive how
he could look up into the heavens and say there is no God."
—Abraham Lincoln, Sixteenth American President

"The visible order of the universe proclaims a supreme intelligence."
—Jean-Jacques Rousseau, French political philosopher

"The visible marks of extraordinary wisdom and power appear
so plainly in all the works of the creation that a rational
creature, who will but seriously reflect on them, cannot miss
the discovery of a Deity."
—John Locke, English political philosopher

"As a house implies a builder, and a garment a weaver, and a door
a carpenter, so does the existence of the Universe imply a Creator."
—Marquis de Vauvenargues, French moralist

"It is impossible to account for the creation of the universe without
the agency of a Supreme Being."
—George Washington, First American President

"From a knowledge of His work, we shall know Him."
—Robert Boyle, Irish chemist

"Nature is the art of God."
—Dante Alighieri, Italian poet

"Those folks had it all figured out. They knew a creation had to
have a Creator. Very basic. But someone, who doesn't believe that
Someone created what they see, won't believe Genesis. And if they
don't believe Genesis, then why would they believe the rest of the
Book? So that, of course, leads them to mock the second coming
of Jesus. The Scriptures are loud and clear that He is coming back!

"Those who doubt God's Hand in His Handiwork need to
ponder some good questions like: How did life originate? How

did the DNA code arise? Where did the first cell come from? Why are the millions of transitional fossils which would prove evolution true still missing? How did a male and a female of each species come into being at the exact same place and at the exact same time with all of their reproductive organs functioning so the species could perpetuate itself? Where did matter come from? Where did space and the universe come from? How did matter get so perfectly organized? How did life come from non-life?

"Those questions can't be answered by an evolutionist, and there is a reason for that: God created! He made it all. Evolution falls like a house of cards when a few questions are asked. Creation truth always trumps the evolutionary lie!

"And probably worst of all are those textbooks that show supposed horse evolution! What a joke. We witnessed all of creation, and we know those beautiful creatures did not evolve but were wonderfully created by the hand of God! *The horse has left the barn* on this one: God created, and evolution was not needed and is not possible!

"And, of course, the final end to all of this is that these folks do not believe in a final Judgment. They do not believe that God is going to judge them. Live and let live. Carpe Diem. Seize the day. Eat, drink, and be merry, for today we live and tomorrow we die.

"They just don't realize that when they die, they will be making an appearance before the throne of God. What a wake-up call that will be for so many of those people. And with that wake-up call, they will not be able to hit the snooze button. Wide awake and meeting their Maker; and sadly, many are not ready or even preparing for that day.

"Maybe even sadder still is that Christians know people are going to face that Judgment, and they are not preparing the lost with the eternal truths of the cross to get them ready for that final day before His throne. This is no time to be lukewarm, which leads me to the next church.

"Laodicea was located on a high plateau and on one of the two biggest trade routes, so they were not invincible. Their biggest problem was their need for water. That was their Achilles heel because it was transported by aqueduct. They had to keep peace with others to protect their water supply. But, of course, peace can be very fleeting. It was also a very wealthy city that was renowned for its eye salve.

"The water had to travel such a great distance to get to them that many times it arrived dirty, polluted, and lukewarm. Not very good to drink, and also not a very good way to live one's life.

"*Laodicea* means 'people rule.' And that was the problem in the church. People ruled instead of Jesus ruling. That typically leads to a worldly and apathetic approach to church. A half-hearted attitude always has a very disastrous ending.

"Jesus identifies Himself as the Truth to the Church of Laodicea. Lukewarm always plays the middle ground. Lukewarm takes the position of compromise. Lukewarm doesn't want to upset the carrot cart. Truth doesn't worry about that. Truth trumps all of that. If the carrots spill, He will make some more of them. Truth always reigns supreme. Truth is always victorious in the end. The question is will people come running to the truth? Lukewarm doesn't cut it when truth shows up on the scene.

"Jesus is standing and knocking on the door of this church. Will they listen? Will they repent? He reproves those He loves. He extends love and acceptance to them. But now, they have a choice. They must decide which direction they will walk: to the cross or away from the cross. The middle ground is not acceptable.

"Christians cannot live incognito lives for Jesus. Indifference is unacceptable. They need to have the same attitude towards the lost that Jesus has for the Laodiceans: all-out truth spoken in all-out love. Nothing else matters.

"Satan will always try to make people blind to truth. He loves false churches. They wind up worrying about the false needs of the congregation. Music, activities, blaring sound systems, theater seating, watered-down truth, theatrical plays, psychology-based teachings, and being seeker-sensitive instead of truth-proclaiming are some of those false needs. And omitting offensive, truthful teachings is always deadly for a church. It is a prescription for lukewarmness that Satan loves to fill. They have the trappings of church, but not the heart of God. The church becomes a business and not much more than that. *Church Inc.* is not what God is looking for. Living for pleasure and self and what I can get from God will never please the Lord.

"Satan will always try to replace truth with lies. He will always try to slip in worldly philosophies and try to get people thinking that the most powerful Document ever written is nothing but myths, fables, legends, and superstitions. No one should buy the lukewarm lie of the Laodiceans, which is lethal for the soul.

"The number one problem in the world today is the rejection of Jesus Christ. Plain and simple. It is the root cause of everything. If people would come to the Lord for salvation and then live for Him, what a gorgeous sight it would be! But we can tell those people are not going to do that. The whoring around after other gods continues. The last church has arrived. The end is near. The world's judgment is about to come to its final conclusion."

"Well, guys, we're finally here. We have arrived. We're at the threshold," Ivory said, glancing at the others. *"You fellas ready? This has been a long time coming. Looks like we will be getting the orders very soon,"* Crimson conferred with his friends.

"Yes, we're ready," Ivory said taking a deep breath. *"This is the reason we were called. This is the reason we've come. And we witnessed it all."*

"Take a last look around, y'all. It's almost go time. Time to wrap it up. We're at the gates. The time is now," Crimson said with finality and resolve.

Chapter 23
The Last Ride

"**W**ords don't do justice to this place," Elap said, surveying the view. "It will be hard to leave, but we have a job to do. And when the Most High tells us to do something, we will do it. No hesitation and no questions asked. We have an assignment, and that assignment will be accomplished.

"Evil is having its heyday. It is having its moment of glory. People are totally immersed in wickedness now. The Heavenly Father is wrapping things up, but people don't realize it. If they had studied the Scriptures, they would have known.

"The defeat of evil is coming. Wickedness is about to be stopped dead in its tracks. The overthrow of evil is on the horizon. The people are clueless to what is about to begin. This is so sad in so many ways; but yet, so necessary.

"Horses walk at roughly 3 to 4 mph. They trot at about 8 to 10 mph. They canter between 10 to 17 mph. But when a horse gallops, that is when it really takes off! Some Quarter Horses can run at speeds of 50 mph! That is what is happening now. The pace has quickened. Time is running out. The finish line is just ahead.

"It is written:

> And I saw when the Lamb opened one of the seals, and I heard, as it were, the noise of thunder, one of the four beasts saying, Come and see. And I saw, and behold a white horse: and he that sat on him had a bow; and a crown was given unto him: and he went forth conquering, and to conquer.

"The time is now, Ivory. Your job is about to commence. War is coming on the world in an unprecedented way. People wouldn't heed God's command to not murder. They wouldn't even heed His command to not hate in their hearts. They have always wanted to conquer. That would put them in the seat of power, or so they thought. The Antichrist thinks he will be doing the conquering. The Final Fuhrer is on the scene, and it is not going to be pretty. He will use every force he can muster to bring the world under his control so it will worship him. But instead, this will end with bringing glory to the One Who shed His blood for the sins of the world!

"But conquering can also have a religious sense to it. False religions abound. The false views of Jesus are seemingly everywhere. They can move at the speed of Secretariat on the Internet and across the airwaves. These are dangerous times, especially when people do not study their Bibles to show themselves approved unto God and get ready for battle.

"A bow is a very precise instrument of war. It will strike exactly where it needs to. No messing around here. God means business. Game time is over.

"The world had a lot of uses for the term *white horse*. It is a slang term for heroin. *White pony* is a slang term for cocaine. None of those drugs will help them at this time. No drug will ever help them escape the reality of what is about to hit them. A white-topped wave or a wave that has a white, broken crest is also known as a *white horse*. They should have recognized the God who made those gorgeous, curling waves. Judgment is coming, and so many are not ready.

"It is time. Ivory, GO!!!

"It is written:

> And when he had opened the second seal, I heard the second beast say, Come and see.
> And there went out another horse that was red: and power was given to him that sat thereon to take peace from the earth, and that they should kill one another: and there was given unto him a great sword.

212

"Amazing power is about to hit planet Earth," Elap continued.

"Redhorse sucker is a type of fish. *REDHORSE Squadrons* is a term that refers to the Rapid Engineer Deployable Heavy Operational Repair Squadron Engineer heavy construction units of the U.S. Air Force. But truly, this horse is going to bring down heavy operations on the people of earth.

"War on an unprecedented scale is about to occur. Like the Holocaust on steroids. It was not pretty the first time, and it will not be pretty this time. The counterfeit peace that the Antichrist brings will now come to naught. It has been a false peace the entire time, but people who have not sought biblical wisdom do not realize that. There will never be true peace without the Prince of Peace. Totally impossible and a colossal waste of time. Interesting, because most men want peace at all costs. We can see that by how they live. They really didn't grasp that life is like a vapor. It is here one minute, and then they are on the other side with the Lord. God has given them His prescription for peace. It is His Son. They have said, 'no thank you.' They will now pay the price.

"Blood is going to be shed. This will not be pretty. They should have chosen the blood of Christ; but now, for many, it will be their own blood that will be spilled. It is a simple choice from our perspective. Always has been.

"It is time. Crimson, GO!!!

"It is written:

> And when he had opened the third seal, I heard the third beast say, Come and see. And I beheld, and lo a black horse; and he that sat on him had a pair of balances in his hand. And I heard a voice in the midst of the four beasts say, A measure of wheat for a penny, and three measures of barley for a penny; and see thou hurt not the oil and the wine.

"Famine will always follow a time of war. Supply chains are broken. People will tend to fend for themselves. Looking out for others is not on the mind of the selfish," Elap had noticed throughout the years.

"The Antichrist is trying to order the world. The balances mean they will be rationing out food supplies, but they will create famine instead. Many people in the western world have not gone to bed hungry before. Those hunger pangs are still there the next morning when the plate is empty. Many take food for granted. That time of plenty will be coming to an end. More power will come to the Antichrist and his cronies as people look to the government for their answers. Just like in the time of Egypt, the Jews went to Pharaoh for their answers. Little do they know, the Antichrist and his followers will be put on the scales, and they will be weighed and found wanting.

"Jeremiah wrote in Lamentations: *'Our skin was black like an oven because of the terrible famine.'* So true. Starvation, disease, and death are taking over.

"*Black horse* is a term for someone you really like. Your ideal partner, but you don't have a chance with them. *Black horse* is also a term for a very potent form of heroin. Sadly, many people really like sin. They like to play with it. They like to dance with it. They think it's their ideal partner, but sin always leaves them high and dry. It leaves them hanging. It will always lead to a lake of fire, unless it is forgiven.

"It is time. Onyx, GO!!!

"It is written:

> And when he had opened the fourth seal, I heard the voice of the fourth beast say, Come and see. And I looked, and behold a pale horse: and his name that sat on him was Death, and Hell followed with him. And power was given unto them over the fourth part of the earth, to kill with sword, and with hunger, and with death, and with the beasts of the earth.

"Sadly, when God is gracious to those people, they tend to pay Him no attention. They only seem to wake up when trouble comes. Major trouble is about to hit them again.

"Pale is the color of death. The overwhelming judgments are taking over, and they are slowly succumbing to death. They are not realizing that death is leading to Hell for most of them. They have rejected Jesus. They have ridiculed and mocked Him. They would not listen to Him, and now they shall reap what they have sown. They had so many chances. They had all the time in the world to repent, and now they will have all the time in eternity to regret their decision to not do so.

"My name is Pale. The other horses liked to have fun with me by saying my name backwards. But even during those humorous times, we knew that serious business was ahead. It was so delightful to see Jesus smile with those kids and with His disciples. He just loves them and their company so much. But there is a time for horseplay, and there is time for serious business. And this serious business will continue until the mission has been accomplished."

"It is time. Pale, GO!!!"

"Chaos ensues on earth. The smaller population is easier for the Antichrist and his forces to control. He thinks he will gain order out of chaos, but it will not be so.

"God set those people up for success through His cross. All they had to do was study the Bible and see the names of the Antichrist, and they would have known. He was called:

THE NAMES OF THE ANTICHRIST

The Seed of the Serpent	The Willful King
The Little Horn	The Man of Sin
The King of Fierce Countenance	The Son of Perdition
The Prince Who Shall Come	The Wicked One
He Who Makes Desolate	The Beast

"Why would anyone follow him to their eternal destruction? Choices have consequences; and now, they will be eternal ones.

"But there was another Person they could have chosen to follow. His names in the Bible are:

THE NAMES OF GOD

ADVOCATE, ALMIGHTY, ALPHA AND OMEGA, AMEN, APOSTLE OF OUR PROFESSION, ARM OF THE LORD, AUTHOR AND FINISHER OF OUR FAITH, AUTHOR OF ETERNAL SALVATION, BEGINNING OF THE CREATION OF GOD, BELOVED SON, BLESSED AND ONLY POTENTATE, BLESSED GOD, BRANCH, BREAD OF LIFE, CAPTAIN OF SALVATION, CHIEF SHEPHERD, CHRIST OF GOD, CONSOLATION OF ISRAEL, CORNERSTONE, COUNSELLOR, CREATOR, DAYSPRING, DELIVERER, DESIRE OF THE NATIONS, DOOR, ELECT OF GOD, EVERLASTING FATHER, FAITHFUL WITNESS, THE FIRST AND THE LAST, FIRST BEGOTTEN OF THE DEAD, FORERUNNER, GLORY OF THE LORD, GOD, GOOD SHEPHERD, GOVERNOR, GREAT HIGH PRIEST, HEAD OF THE CHURCH, HEIR OF ALL THINGS, HOLY CHILD, HOLY ONE, HOLY ONE OF GOD, HOLY ONE OF ISRAEL, HORN OF SALVATION, I AM, IMAGE OF GOD, IMMANUEL, JEHOVAH, JESUS, JESUS OF NAZARETH, JUDGE OF ISRAEL, THE JUST ONE, KING, KING OF THE AGES, KING OF THE JEWS, KING OF KINGS, KING OF SAINTS, LAST ADAM, LAWGIVER, LAMB, LAMB OF GOD, LEADER AND COMMANDER, THE LIFE, LIGHT OF THE WORLD, LION OF THE TRIBE OF JUDAH, LORD OF ALL, LORD OF GLORY, LORD OF LORDS, THE LORD OUR RIGHTEOUSNESS, MAN OF SORROWS, MEDIATOR, MESSENGER OF THE COVENANT, MESSIAH, MIGHTY GOD, MIGHTY ONE, MORNING STAR, NAZARENE, ONLY BEGOTTEN SON, OUR PASSOVER, PRINCE OF LIFE, PRINCE OF KINGS, PRINCE OF PEACE, PROPHET, REDEEMER, RESURRECTION AND LIFE, ROCK, ROOT OF DAVID, ROSE OF SHARON, SAVIOUR, SHEPHERD AND BISHOP OF SOULS, SHILOH, SON OF THE BLESSED, SON OF DAVID, SON OF GOD, SON OF THE HIGHEST, SUN OF RIGHTEOUSNESS, TRUE LIGHT, TRUE VINE, TRUTH, WITNESS, WORD, WORD OF GOD.

"These two lists of names make the differences really simple to see. Choose your list. Choose who you want to follow. Go through the names again. It is a very easy decision to make; and many people have, to this point, made the wrong and eternally horrible choice.

"Sadly, some of these people will not accept the real Savior, but instead will follow a false one. And even sadder, they will make war with the Lamb until the end. The stench of the fornication of the world has risen to the nostrils of God. Time to close this last chapter. Time to show them, face to face, Who they have been missing. Who they have rejected. Who had all of the answers. Who was their only hope. Who gave them the breath of life, and they wanted nothing to do with Him. Who died for their sins, and they didn't want His forgiveness. Who loved them unconditionally all the days of their lives.

"There were a lot of *lasts* down there on planet Earth that draw attention to the end of something: last stand, last call, last one is it, last night, last time, Last Mohican, last straw, last act, last word, last bastion of hope, last chance, last dance, last curtain call, down to the last drop, last but not least, last hurrah, last of the big spenders, fun while it lasted, at long last, he who laughs last, last will and testament, last gasp, last one out, the last resort, last ditch effort, last survivor, last crusader, last resting place, last generation, last goodbye, last judgment, last kiss, last holdout, last minute, last details, last man standing, down to the last man, last meal, last year, last mile, last resort, last name, last rites, last wishes, last seen, last song, last time around, last waltz, last week's news, last breath, on its last legs, and famous last words. My favorite, though, is the Last Supper. But now, it is time for the last roundup. It is time to gather all of the people of the world together for eternity. Their last chance is just about up.

"My name is Pure. I am uncontaminated by the things of the world. My job is about to commence. It is now time for *The Last Ride*."

 "IT IS TIME!! PURE, *GO!!!!!*"

And I saw heaven opened, and behold a white horse; and he that sat upon him was called Faithful and True, and in righteousness he doth judge and make war.

His eyes were as a flame of fire, and on his head were many crowns; and he had a name written, that no man knew, but he himself.

And he was clothed with a vesture dipped in blood: and his name is called The Word of God.

And the armies which were in heaven followed him upon white horses, clothed in fine linen, white and clean.

And out of his mouth goeth a sharp sword, that with it he should smite the nations: and he shall rule them with a rod of iron: and he treadeth the winepress of the fierceness and wrath of Almighty God.

And he hath on his vesture and on his thigh a name written, KING OF KINGS, AND LORD OF LORDS.

And I saw an angel standing in the sun; and he cried with a loud voice, saying to all the fowls that fly in the midst of heaven, Come and gather yourselves together unto the supper of the great God;

That ye may eat the flesh of kings, and the flesh of captains, and the flesh of mighty men, and the flesh of horses, and of them that sit on them, and the flesh of all men, both free and bond, both small and great.

And I saw the beast, and the kings of the earth, and their armies, gathered together to make war against him that sat on the horse, and against his army.

And the beast was taken, and with him the false prophet that wrought miracles before him, with which he deceived them that had received the mark of the beast, and them that worshipped his image. These both were cast alive into a lake of fire burning with brimstone.

And the remnant were slain with the sword of him that sat upon the horse, which sword proceeded out of his mouth: and all the fowls were filled with their flesh.

And I saw an angel come down from heaven, having the key of the bottomless pit and a great chain in his hand.

And he laid hold on the dragon, that old serpent, which is the Devil, and Satan, and bound him a thousand years,

And cast him into the bottomless pit, and shut him up, and set a seal upon him, that he should deceive the nations no more, till the thousand years should be fulfilled: and after that he must be loosed a little season.

And I saw thrones, and they sat upon them, and judgment was given unto them: and I saw the souls of them that were beheaded for the witness of Jesus, and for the word of God, and which had not worshipped the beast, neither his image, neither had received his mark upon their foreheads, or in their hands; and they lived and reigned with Christ a thousand years.

But the rest of the dead lived not again until the thousand years were finished. This is the first resurrection.

Blessed and holy is he that hath part in the first resurrection: on such the second death hath no power, but they shall be priests of God and of Christ, and shall reign with him a thousand years.

And when the thousand years are expired, Satan shall be loosed out of his prison,

And shall go out to deceive the nations which are in the four quarters of the earth, Gog, and Magog, to gather them together to battle: the number of whom is as the sand of the sea.

And they went up on the breadth of the earth, and compassed the camp of the saints about, and the beloved city: and fire came down from God out of heaven, and devoured them.

And the devil that deceived them was cast into the lake of fire and brimstone, where the beast and the false prophet are, and shall be tormented day and night for ever and ever.

And I saw a great white throne, and him that sat on it, from whose face the earth and the heaven fled away; and there was found no place for them.

And I saw the dead, small and great, stand before God; and the books were opened:

and another book was opened, which is the book of life: and the dead were judged out of those things which were written in the books, according to their works.

And the sea gave up the dead which were in it; and death and hell delivered up the dead which were in them: and they were judged every man according to their works.

And death and hell were cast into the lake of fire. This is the second death.

And whosoever was not found written in the book of life was cast into the lake of fire.

And I saw a new heaven and a new earth: for the first heaven and the first earth were passed away; and there was no more sea.

And I John saw the holy city, new Jerusalem, coming down from God out of heaven, prepared as a bride adorned for her husband.

And I heard a great voice out of heaven saying, Behold, the tabernacle of God is with men, and he will dwell with them, and they shall be his people, and God himself shall be with them, and be their God.

And God shall wipe away all tears from their eyes; and there shall be no more death, neither sorrow, nor crying, neither shall there be any more pain: for the former things are passed away.

And he that sat upon the throne said, Behold, I make all things new. And he said unto me, Write: for these words are true and faithful.

And he said unto me, It is done. I am Alpha and Omega, the beginning and the end. I will give unto him that is athirst of the fountain of the water of life freely.

He that overcometh shall inherit all things; and I will be his God, and he shall be my son.

But the fearful, and unbelieving, and the abominable, and murderers, and whoremongers, and sorcerers, and idolaters, and all liars, shall have their part in the lake which burneth with fire and brimstone: which is the second death.

And there came unto me one of the seven angels which

had the seven vials full of the seven last plagues, and talked with me, saying, Come hither, I will shew thee the bride, the Lamb's wife.

And he carried me away in the spirit to a great and high mountain, and shewed me that great city, the holy Jerusalem, descending out of heaven from God,

Having the glory of God: and her light was like unto a stone most precious, even like a jasper stone, clear as crystal;

And had a wall great and high, and had twelve gates, and at the gates twelve angels, and names written thereon, which are the names of the twelve tribes of the children of Israel:

On the east three gates; on the north three gates; on the south three gates; and on the west three gates.

And the wall of the city had twelve foundations, and in them the names of the twelve apostles of the Lamb.

And he that talked with me had a golden reed to measure the city, and the gates thereof, and the wall thereof.

And the city lieth foursquare, and the length is as large as the breadth: and he measured the city with the reed, twelve thousand furlongs. The length and the breadth and the height of it are equal.

And he measured the wall thereof, an hundred and forty and four cubits, according to the measure of a man, that is, of the angel.

And the building of the wall of it was of jasper: and the city was pure gold, like unto clear glass.

And the foundations of the wall of the city were garnished with all manner of precious stones. The first foundation was jasper; the second, sapphire; the third, a chalcedony; the fourth, an emerald;

The fifth, sardonyx; the sixth, sardius; the seventh, chrysolyte; the eighth, beryl; the ninth, a topaz; the tenth, a chrysoprasus; the eleventh, a jacinth; the twelfth, an amethyst.

And the twelve gates were twelve pearls: every several gate was of one pearl: and the street of the city was pure gold, as it were transparent glass.

And I saw no temple therein: for the Lord God Almighty and the Lamb are the temple of it.

And the city had no need of the sun, neither of the moon, to shine in it: for the glory of God did lighten it, and the Lamb is the light thereof.

And the nations of them which are saved shall walk in the light of it: and the kings of the earth do bring their glory and honour into it.

And the gates of it shall not be shut at all by day: for there shall be no night there.

And they shall bring the glory and honour of the nations into it.

And there shall in no wise enter into it any thing that defileth, neither whatsoever worketh abomination, or maketh a lie: but they which are written in the Lamb's book of life.

And he shewed me a pure river of water of life, clear as crystal, proceeding out of the throne of God and of the Lamb.

In the midst of the street of it, and on either side of the river, was there the tree of life, which bare twelve manner of fruits, and yielded her fruit every month: and the leaves of the tree were for the healing of the nations.

And there shall be no more curse: but the throne of God and of the Lamb shall be in it; and his servants shall serve him:

And they shall see his face; and his name shall be in their foreheads.

And there shall be no night there; and they need no candle, neither light of the sun; for the Lord God giveth them light: and they shall reign for ever and ever.

And he said unto me, These sayings are faithful and true: and the Lord God of the holy prophets sent his angel to shew unto his servants the things which must shortly be done.

Behold, I come quickly: blessed is he that keepeth the sayings of the prophecy of this book.

And I John saw these things, and heard them. And when I had heard and seen, I fell down to worship before the feet of the angel which shewed me these things.

Then saith he unto me, See thou do it not: for I am thy fellowservant, and of thy brethren the prophets, and of them which keep the sayings of this book: worship God.

And he saith unto me, Seal not the sayings of the prophecy of this book: for the time is at hand.

He that is unjust, let him be unjust still: and he which is filthy, let him be filthy still: and he that is righteous, let him be righteous still: and he that is holy, let him be holy still.

And, behold, I come quickly; and my reward is with me, to give every man according as his work shall be.

I am Alpha and Omega, the beginning and the end, the first and the last.

Blessed are they that do his commandments, that they may have right to the tree of life, and may enter in through the gates into the city.

For without are dogs, and sorcerers, and whoremongers, and murderers, and idolaters, and whosoever loveth and maketh a lie.

I Jesus have sent mine angel to testify unto you these things in the churches. I am the root and the offspring of David, and the bright and morning star.

And the Spirit and the bride say, Come. And let him that heareth say, Come. And let him that is athirst come. And whosoever will, let him take the water of life freely.

For I testify unto every man that heareth the words of the prophecy of this book, If any man shall add unto these things, God shall add unto him the plagues that are written in this book:

And if any man shall take away from the words of the book of this prophecy, God shall take away his part out of the book of life, and out of the holy city, and from the things which are written in this book.

He which testifieth these things saith, Surely I come quickly. Amen. Even so, come, Lord Jesus.

The grace of our Lord Jesus Christ be with you all. Amen.

Mark Cahill has a business degree from Auburn University, where he was an honorable mention Academic All-American in basketball. He has worked in the business world at IBM and in various management positions, and he taught high school for four years. Mark now speaks to thousands of people a year at churches, conferences, camps, retreats, and other events. He has also appeared on numerous radio and television shows.

Mark's favorite thing to do is to go out and meet people to find out what they believe and why they believe it. You can find Mark at malls, concerts, art and music festivals, airports, beaches, sporting events, bar sections of towns, college campuses, and wherever people gather doing just that.

> To arrange a speaking engagement,
> contact the **Ambassador Agency**
> at 615-370-4700 or
> www.ambassadoragency.com

•

To order additional books or resources,
or to receive a free e-newsletter, visit:
www.markcahill.org

•

> Contact Mark Cahill at:
> P.O. Box 81, Stone Mountain, GA 30086
> 800-NETS-158 / 800-638-7158
> Email: mark@markcahill.org